THE STRANGE WORLD
OF THOMAS HARRIS

THE STRANGE WORLD OF THOMAS HARRIS

DAVID SEXTON

✱ SHORT BOOKS

FRONT LINES

First published in 2001 by
Short Books
15 Highbury Terrace
London N5 1UP

A CIP catalogue record for this book
is available from the British Library.

ISBN 0 571 20845 2

Printed in Great Britain by
Bookmarque Ltd, Croydon, Surrey

Mais parmi les chacals, les panthères, les lices,
Les singes, les scorpions, les vautours, les serpents,
Les monstres glapissants, hurlants, grognants, rampants,
Dans la ménagerie infâme de nos vices,

Il en est un plus laid, plus méchant, plus immonde!
Quoiqu'il ne pousse ni grands gestes ni grands cris,
Il ferait volontiers de la terre un débris
Et dans un bâillement avalerait le monde;

C'est l'Ennui! – l'oeil chargé d'un pleur involontaire,
Il rêve d'échafauds en fumant son houka.
Tu le connais, lecteur, ce monstre délicat,
– Hypocrite lecteur, – mon semblable, – mon frère!
Baudelaire, 'Au Lecteur', *Les Fleurs du Mal*

'If you want to understand the artist, look at his work.'
John Douglas, *Mindhunter: Inside the FBI Elite Serial Crime Unit*

'If He's up there, He just loves it, Officer Starling. Typhoid and swans – it all comes from the same place.'
Thomas Harris, *The Silence of the Lambs*

One: Introduction

Our first sight of the doctor is through his handiwork. A signature on a living body. He has left a scar on the stomach of Will Graham, the FBI agent who caught him. 'It was finger-width and raised and never tanned. It ran down from his left hip-bone and turned up to notch his rib-cage on the other side.

'Dr Hannibal Lecter did that with a linoleum knife.'

Dr Lecter, we learn, is known in the tabloids as 'Hannibal the Cannibal'. He is the second 'psychopath' that Graham caught and he nearly killed him.

Lecter is not mentioned again for 40 pages of this novel, *Red Dragon*. In the meantime we follow Will Graham's visit to the scene of the latest murders by another serial killer and discover Graham's uncomfortable ability to empathise with madness. 'He viewed his own mentality as grotesque but useful, like a chair made of antlers. There was nothing he could do about it.'

Then, in conversation with another detective, Graham discloses a little more about Lecter. He killed nine people before he was captured, 'nine that we know of... He did it because he liked it. Still does. Dr Lecter is not crazy, in any common way we think of being crazy. He did some hideous things because he enjoyed them. But he can function perfectly when he wants to... He has no remorse or guilt at all.'

The psychologists say he's a sociopath 'because they don't know what else to call him'. Graham thinks of him simply as a monster, 'one of those pitiful things that are born in hospitals from time to time'. He prefers to believe that it was luck that allowed him to catch Lecter, not empathy. But he decides, none the less, that he needs Lecter's opinion on the current case. He goes to interview him at Chesapeake State Hospital for the Criminally Insane.

But before we finally meet the doctor, there is more of the legend. The hospital's chief of staff, Dr Frederick Chilton, tells Graham that Lecter has attacked a nurse in the hospital, while being given an electrocardiogram. 'The nurse was very quick and strong. She managed to save one of her eyes... Do you notice the strange thing? His pulse never got over 85. Even when he tore out her tongue.'

Dr Chilton has tried to study Lecter. 'You know, when Lecter was first captured we thought he might provide us with a singular opportunity to study a pure sociopath... It's so rare to get one alive.' But he has got nowhere with this study. Lecter, on the other hand, has continued to publish 'brilliant pieces' in the psychiatric journals from his cell.

At last we see this monster for ourselves. He's asleep. 'Alexandre Dumas's *Le Grand Dictionnaire de Cuisine* was open on his chest.' Hannibal Lecter is a great reader. He'll cook from this book in due course. Now he opens his eyes and the first thing he does is to comment on how Will Graham smells. 'That's the same atrocious aftershave you wore in court.'

Lecter is very attentive to smell. Years later, near the end of *Hannibal*, he will tell Clarice Starling, before he serves her the brains of her enemy: 'Clarice, dinner appeals to taste and smell, the oldest senses and the closest to the centre of the mind. Taste and smell are housed in parts of the mind that precede pity, and pity has no place at my table.' He is alluding to Dante's *Inferno* (Canto XX, 27–28): 'There is no place for pity here' (in the translation by Robert Pinsky, used by Thomas Harris).

Every aspect of Hannibal Lecter's appearance is remarkable. His eyes are 'maroon and they reflect the light redly, in tiny points'. He is 'a small, lithe man. Very neat.' His teeth are small and white. He seldom holds his head upright, he tilts it 'as though he were screwing an augur of curiosity into your face'. Later, we are to learn that he has six perfectly formed fingers on his left hand, the rarest form of polydactyly.

Hannibal Lecter's mind is no less strange. He combines complete insight into others with a complete lack of sympathy for them. He knows why Graham has come to see him in his hospital cell. 'You just came here to look at me. Just to get the old scent again, didn't you? Why don't you just smell yourself?' As Graham leaves, Lecter tells him the truth he cannot bear: 'The reason you caught me is that *we're just alike.*'

We are to find that another of Lecter's unusual characteristics is that he never lies.

***

Thus is introduced the most powerful character in modern melodrama. Thomas Harris has created many other characters. Each novel introduces a new murderer – Francis Dolarhyde in *Red Dragon*, Jame Gumb in *The Silence of the Lambs* and Mason Verger in *Hannibal*. Jack Crawford of the Behavioral Science Unit at the FBI Academy in Quantico, Virginia, appears in all the books, sending out both Will Graham and Clarice Starling to fight monsters. But it is Hannibal Lecter who is known all over the world. He is as recognisable now as Sherlock Holmes, one of his fictional forebears. Lecter has become an immortal. As the deliberation of the presentation shows, Harris knew from the start what effect he wanted to create.

The scale of Harris's success has been astounding, given his method of operation. He has published just four books, at increasingly long intervals. The first, *Black Sunday* of 1975, was apprentice work and were it not by Harris would no longer be in print. When he wrote it, Harris did not yet know the nature of his talent. It's no more than pretty good. However, it was quickly made into a film, also called *Black Sunday* (1977), directed by John Frankenheimer, and its profits gave Harris the freedom to change, to discover what kind of writer he really might be. The transformation he wrought on himself was in its way as radical as any attempted by his deranged killers. The possibilities of change became one of his subjects. *Red Dragon*, his first masterpiece, did not appear until six years later, in 1981. *The Silence of the Lambs*, a still finer novel, took seven years more. *Hannibal*, the longest, a book that has choked some of his most avid fans, was some 11 years in the making.

There's a good reason for these delays. The books are original in the sense that they have changed the very possibilities of the form. They are more intricately constructed and, line by line, paragraph by paragraph, are better written than anything else in the field. It's understandable that they take a long time to make.

The sales have been huge, of course. Harris started to make big money with the publication of *Red Dragon* when the paperback rights were sold for over $1 million to Bantam in the United States and for another £115,000 in Britain to Corgi. *The Silence of the Lambs* has now sold some 12 million copies worldwide. For many months after the release of the movie on 4 February 1991, the two books dominated the bestseller lists on both sides of the Atlantic. The film of *The Silence of the Lambs* cost $13.5 million to make but then took over $100 million in its first year, eventually grossing far more, as well as receiving five Oscars, including best picture, best actor and best actress.

In 1988 Harris's American editor, Carole Baron, signed a two-book deal with him for $5.2 million. Eleven years later, the initial global print-run of *Hannibal* was a million copies. Half a million were printed in America, 150,000 in Britain, where it sold out on the first day, 8 June 1999.

The hardback of *Hannibal* went on to sell several million around the world; the sales of the paperback may eventually rival those of *The Silence of the Lambs*. Harris received a record $9 million for the film rights of *Hannibal* and Ridley Scott's rapidly produced movie took $58 million in America on its first three days, and £6 million in Britain, despite receiving only moderate reviews.

But Harris's influence has been even more remarkable than his sales. He has created a new fascination in popular culture with serial killers – and with the 'profilers' who pursue them. Even the two FBI men on whose work with serial killers Thomas Harris drew, Robert Ressler and John Douglas, have been able to pursue successful careers as authors in the wake of this boom. And many, many thriller-writers and film-makers have made profitable enterprises out of emulating Harris. Among Harris's more accomplished admirers are James Ellroy, John Connolly and T. Jefferson Parker. *Seven* (1995) was perhaps the most incisive film to be launched on the serial-killer wave; others included *Basic Instinct* (1992), *Natural Born Killers* (1994) and *Copycat* (1995).

Such was the impact of *The Silence of the Lambs* that its one unforgettable autopsy scene – showing a woman confronting a corpse on the dissecting table, and ultimately forcing her to face the man responsible for the murder – spurred on a whole genre of female forensic-pathologist books, movies and television series. *PostMortem*, Patricia D. Cornwell's first Kay Scarpetta novel to be published (her fourth attempt at a book) finally appeared in 1990, after having been rejected by seven publishers. Such has been Cornwell's success that she now has her own follower, Kathy Reichs, who began her series of novels about a female forensic pathologist with the choicely titled *Déjà Dead*.

Clarice Starling had her part to play in *The X-Files*, too. 'Without Clarice, there'd be no Agent Scully, or at least no Agent Scully so wise or – and this is the thing – so good,' says Joyce Millman of *Salon*, the online magazine. Then there has been all that 'profiler' fiction, including the gargantuan *Cracker*. But none of these entrepreneurs has anything like Harris's art; none has created another Lecter.

Between the writing of *Black Sunday* and *Red Dragon*, Harris found his voice. To do this he needed to learn a good deal about both serial killers and the men and women who hunt them.

Robert Ressler says in his memoir of his work for the FBI, *Whoever Fights Monsters*, that he only coined the term 'serial killer' in the mid-1970s. The FBI Academy at Quantico had just recently opened and its Behavioral Science Unit, developing the art of profiling offenders, was in its earliest stages. Ressler taught there, his subjects 'ranging from abnormal psych to inter-viewing techniques'.

At the time, he recalls, 'killings such as those of the "Son of Sam" killer David Berkowitz in New York were invariably labelled "stranger killings". This term didn't seem appropriate to me, however, for sometimes killers do know their victims. Various other terms had also been used, but none hit the nail on the head. I'd been invited to participate in a week of lectures at Bramshill, the British police academy, and while there I took the opportunity to attend the other seminars and lectures. In one of them, a man was discussing what the Brits called "crimes in series" – a series of rapes, burglaries, arsons, murders. That seemed a highly appropriate way of characterising those who do one murder, then another and another in a fairly repetitive way, and so in my classes at Quantico and elsewhere I began referring to "serial killers".'

Ressler adds: 'Now that I look back on that naming event, I think that what was also in my mind were the serial adventures we used to see on Saturdays at the movies (the one I liked best was *The Phantom*). Each week, you'd be lured back to see another episode, because at the end of each one there was a cliffhanger. In dramatic terms, this wasn't a satisfactory ending, because it increased, not lessened, the tension. The same dissatisfaction occurs in the minds of serial killers... They are obsessed with a fantasy, and they have what we must call non-fulfilled experiences that become part of the fantasy and push them on towards the next killing. That's the real meaning behind the term "serial killer".'

Even if Harris had never studied the work being done by Ressler and Douglas, he would doubtless have become a fine writer. But he would have been a different one. It's also true that it was his own nature, long pre-existing, that enabled him to seize the opportunity so brilliantly. To understand that, we must look earlier in his life

Two: No Interviews

There is this difficulty: he doesn't give interviews. He has this in common with J. D. Salinger, Thomas Pynchon and, most famously, Samuel Beckett, who told one applicant that he had 'no views to inter'. But it's still a mite unusual for a bestselling thriller writer to take such a stance. His publishers have learned to live with such intransigence; even to embrace it. For the publication of *Hannibal*, Random House issued a flat statement: 'Thomas Harris is not available for interview and will not be coming to the UK for publication.'

There's a much-repeated story that Harris was offended by an interviewer who, in 1984, suggested that Hannibal Lecter was really Harris himself, or that at least he had to be a bit of a psychopath to write about them so well; so offended that he decided there and then never to speak to a journalist again. This seems unlikely to be correct. For one thing, Harris is not so naive as to find the idea that he has drawn on his own imagination in creating his characters surprising.

For another, Harris knew about journalists already. He used to be one. He had already given, in *Red Dragon*, as savage a picture of journalism as any in fiction, in the person of Freddy Lounds of the *National Tattler*. Lounds, we are told, had covered the original Lecter case. He did the quickie paperback. When Will Graham was injured, 'Lounds had come into the hospital room while Graham was asleep. He flipped back the sheet and shot a picture of Graham's temporary colostomy. The paper ran it retouched with a black square covering Graham's groin. The caption said "Crazy Guts Cop".'

We are told that Lounds had the qualities of a good reporter: 'intelligence, guts and the good eye'. But, 'In Lounds was the lunging need to be noticed that is often miscalled ego. Lounds was lumpy and ugly and small. He had buckteeth and his rat eyes had the sheen of spit on asphalt.' For ten years, Lounds worked in straight journalism. Then he realised he was never going to be sent to the White House. 'He saw that his publishers would wear his legs out, use him until it was time for him to become a broken-down old drunk manning a dead-end desk, drifting inevitably towards cirrhosis or a mattress fire.'

Lounds has a grotesque epiphany, as so many of Harris's characters do. He sees an older reporter taking dictation. 'Dictation was the glue factory for old reporters on the paper where Freddy worked. Frank Larkin was 55, but he looked 70. He was oyster-eyed and he went to his locker every half-hour for a drink. Freddy could smell him from where he sat.' Then Larkin asks the news editor, a woman, to get him a Kotex from the machine in the ladies room. He has to use them on his bleeding behind. Freddy stops typing.

Freddy joins the *National Tattler* as Cancer Editor. The magazine has discovered that a 'NEW CURE FOR CANCER' or 'CANCER MIRACLE DRUG' headline boosts its supermarket sales by 22.3 per cent. 'The standard story featured an optimistic five paragraphs in ten-point type, then a drop to eight point, then to six point before mentioning that the "miracle drug" was unavailable or that animal research was "just beginning".' (It is one of the legacies of Harris's time in newspapers that he is attentive to lettering. In *Hannibal*, Lecter, who writes a perfect copperplate himself, contemplates a copy of the *National Tattler* in his private chapel: 'The type is 72-

point Railroad Gothic. It says: "DEATH ANGEL: CLARICE STARLING, THE FBI'S KILLING MACHINE".')

In *Red Dragon*, Freddy Lounds is duped into publishing an article in which Will Graham taunts the murderer, the Dragon, in an attempt to lure him out. Freddy has his picture taken with Graham at FBI headquarters in front of a gun rack. He's planning another instant paperback when the perpetrator is arrested, and has already finished '50,000 words of solid background' and attracted the interest of Hollywood. 'His agent talked very big numbers.'

What happens instead is that the Dragon catches Lounds in a car park and chloroforms him. Lounds wakes to find himself in the Dragon's presence, glued to a chair from head to foot. '"What am I doing here?" The question shrill at the end.

'The answer came from far behind him. "Atoning, Mr Lounds."'

The Dragon has been reading his journalism. 'Why do you write lies, Mr Lounds? Why do you say I'm crazy? Answer now.' Lounds makes the Dragon his best offer. 'I'd do a big true story... Anything you want to say. Describe you any way you want, or no description, no description.'

Lounds has realised that if he sees the Dragon he will not be allowed to live. The Dragon insists. 'Oh, but you must, Mr Lounds. You're a reporter. You're here to report. When I turn you around, open your eyes and look at me. If you won't open them yourself, I'll staple your eyelids to your forehead.'

The Dragon shows Lounds his slides of his murder scenes. 'Do you see?' And returns to Lounds's lies. 'Will you tell the truth now? About Me. My Work. My Becoming. My Art, Mr Lounds. Is this Art?' 'Art,' replies the journalist.

Then the Dragon bites Lounds's lips off. This is a specific cruelty for Harris who always notices mouths and speech; who has equipped both Francis Dolarhyde and Mason Verger with deformities of the mouth and defects of speech. (In *Hannibal*'s final scene, on the other hand, it is pointedly and strangely said of Clarice Starling in the Buenos Aires opera house: 'She seemed animated and in expert control of her coral mouth.') Lounds is dumped back at the *Tattler* and appallingly burned in the process. Before he dies he manages, without lips, to say, 'Graham set ne uh. Cunt tut his hand on ne in the ticture like a hucking tet.' That is where Harris places journalists in his Inferno.

So it seems unlikely that Harris will be giving any satisfying interviews – 'Yep, it's me, I'm Lecter' – any time soon. He told one journalist in 1991: 'It's true I don't do interviews. And I haven't in 15 years. I think it's better to try to put everything in the books, you know... I just work and I try to put the things in my books that I want to say. That's about the size of it.' He has used a very similar form of words to every other journalist who has managed to track him down.

After the delivery of the *Hannibal* manuscript in March 1999, Caroline Graham, a journalist, got him on the phone: 'I really can't start giving interviews now. I never have and I never will. I thank you kindly for your interest. But I wish to allow my work to speak for itself.' Undeterred, she called on him in person, to be told again: 'I'm not being reclusive, but I made a decision many years ago not to speak publicly about my work. It's ironic because I used to be a journalist and I understand that people have a fascination with me and my work. I am very appreciative of people's interest. But I prefer to live my life quietly and not get involved in all that. I enjoy what I do and I enjoy my life. Let's leave it at that, shall we?'

Mort Janklow, Harris's long-standing agent, put it this way: 'If you delivered a cheque here for a million dollars, he would not give you a three-cent interview. I just want you to understand how ludicrous the request is.' How could an agent put it more forcefully? Five million, maybe.

In *Hannibal*, even a ruthless killer finds the media

difficult to endure: 'Had Margot Verger known the raw ablative tension suffered by the principals in a media-ridden homicide, she might never have stuffed the eel down her brother's throat.' Ablative means 'removing, taking away from'. This is a sentence that might just reflect Harris's opinion about his part as a principal in media-ridden homicide fiction. On the other hand, he has put what he wants to say in his books and we are invited to find it there. Fair do's.

In *Mindhunter: Inside the FBI Elite Serial Crime Unit,* the FBI profiler John Douglas says: 'If you want to understand the artist, look at his work. That's what I always tell my people. You can't claim to understand or appreciate Picasso without studying his paintings. The successful serial killers plan their work as carefully as a painter plans a canvas. They consider what they do their "art", and they keep refining it as they go along.' So do the successful serial novelists.

Of Harris's four novels, three give a coherent picture of the world he inhabits in his imagination. He has also put his name to just a few carefully thought-out statements. That'll do. It is, after all, only for these books that we want to know about Harris in the first place. We might just say: he can be profiled from the scenes of these crime books.

We have some facts and can make some inferences.

Three: The Background

Thomas Harris was born in 1940 in Jackson, Tennessee. His father, William Thomas Harris Jr., was an electrical engineer who worked for the Tennessee Valley Authority. His mother Polly, then 22, was a high-school chemistry and biology teacher.

Tennessee is revisited in *The Silence of the Lambs*. Memphis is where Catherine Baker Martin is abducted by Jame Gumb and where Hannibal Lecter escapes the custody of Officers Pembry and Boyle. '"Strikes me he's pretty much a broke-dick," Boyle confided to Pembry after they had Dr Lecter secure in his cell. "He won't be no trouble if he don't flip out."' Both die.

Thomas Harris was an only child. So were the murderers of his first three books: Michael Lander, Francis Dolarhyde and Jame Gumb. With the appearance of *Hannibal*, though, we know that Hannibal Lecter had a younger sister, Mischa. She was, according to *Hannibal*, killed and eaten in 1944.

Early in *The Silence of the Lambs* it is mentioned in passing that Clarice Starling had a brother – 'And suddenly her father's voice, speaking to her with his hand on her brother's shoulder, "If you can't play without squawling, Clarice, go on to the house"' – but he never again features. A little later she remembers her mother talking of her 'brothers and sister'. In her disclosure to Lecter, she mentions that she was the eldest of the children. But Clarice is separated from her family at ten and she ends up in an orphanage. None of her siblings is there for her in *Hannibal*. She is alone, too.

In *Hannibal*, the asinine psychologist Dr Doemling points out: 'Lecter was an orphan, like Clarice Starling... What a common experience of being an orphan gives Dr Lecter is simply a better ability to understand her, and ultimately control her.'

In Harris's world, it is normal to be alone, whether by accident of birth or later realisation. Francis Dolarhyde in *Red Dragon*: 'He had known since the age of nine that essentially he was alone and that he would always be alone, a conclusion more common to the forties. Now, in his forties, he was seized by a fantasy life with the brilliance and freshness and immediacy of childhood. It took him a step beyond Alone. At a time when other men first see and fear their isolation, Dolarhyde's became understandable to him: he was alone because he was Unique.'

When Thomas was still a baby, the Harris family moved back to his father's home, Rich, Mississippi. On his return from war service, William Thomas Harris took up farming, in a small way. Though he was charming, by all reports, he didn't make a good farmer and the family had financial problems. He was too 'easygoing' and became increasingly withdrawn; it was Mrs Harris who was the determined one.

William Thomas Harris Jr. died on 1 May 1980, confirms one of the two undertakers in Clarksdale, the county town. Recently, Harris has linked the creation of *Red Dragon* and Hannibal Lecter with the 18 months he spent back in Rich at this time. *Red Dragon* was published in 1981. He dedicated his next book, *The Silence of the Lambs*, 'To the memory of my father'.

Clarice Starling's attempt to live up to her image of her murdered father is one of the central themes of *The Silence of the Lambs* (and indeed *Hannibal*). It is part of her bond with the victim, Catherine Martin. 'She wondered if Catherine tried to please her father when she was little. She wondered what Catherine was doing when they came and told her that her father was dead, of a heart attack at 42. Starling was positive Catherine missed him. Missing your father, the common wound, made Starling feel close to this young woman.'

When Clarice shoots Jame Gumb in the darkness, there's a specific reason why she knows that he is dying: 'A gurgle, a rattle and the whistling stopped. Starling knew that sound too. She'd heard it once before, at the hospital when her father died.' When at the very end, her boss Jack Crawford, just widowed himself, is congratulating her, there is this peculiarly affecting remark: 'He managed to hail her from his berg of grief: "Starling, your father sees you."' It is what she needs to hear, he has understood; wanting, as he does, his late wife still to be seeing him.

But, in *Hannibal*, it becomes apparent that Clarice Starling is imprisoned in the respect she has for her father, and ultimately she learns that he was not as she has idealised him. 'He got killed and left us because he was too goddamned stupid,' she eventually complains to Lecter under hypnosis.

'Starling is a big girl to be fucking her daddy even if she is southern,' jeers her nemesis in the FBI, Krendler, shortly before his lobotomy. But by then Hannibal has already brought Clarice her father's bones and after that practical demonstration of his place in the scheme of things, she's not moved by the insult.

Thomas Harris, for his part, being a man, is a mother's boy, and he has an acute grasp of what it is to be a mother and a son. In the back story we are given in *Red Dragon*, Francis Dolarhyde's mother screams when she sees his deformed face at four days old and abandons him. At a year and half, he goes to a foundling home, followed by an orphanage. At five, he is removed by his grandmother, whose dentures he is later to wear to such ill-effect. When she is hospitalised, his mother reluctantly takes him back but only for a month. As an adult, 'he does not think of his mother's house'.

The Dragon preys upon whole families. As he watches the home movies from which he selects his victims, it is always the mother of the happy family on whom he focuses. 'A close-up. Mother turns and strikes a pose for the camera with an arch smile, her hand at the back of her neck. She is quite lovely. There is a cameo at her throat. Dolarhyde freezes the frame.'

In *The Silence of the Lambs*, Jame Gumb's back story, held until after his death, is that he was placed in a foster home at the age of two. When he was ten, his grandparents took him home. At 12, he killed them. He obsessively watches tiny clips of video footage that he believes to be of his mother and immediately after hugs his poodle tight: 'Oh Precious. Come here to Mommy. Mommy's going to be so beautiful.' He believes that he can become his mother by putting on a woman's skin.

Throughout *The Silence of the Lambs*, Gumb's madness is contrasted with the pain of his victim's mother, Senator Martin. When Lecter meets her, he asks suddenly:

'"Did you nurse Catherine?"

"Pardon me? Did I..."

"Did you breast-feed her?"

"Yes."

"Thirsty work, isn't it...?"

'When her pupils darkened, Dr Lecter took a single sip of her pain and found it exquisite.'

In *Hannibal*, Clarice Starling in the very first chapter is forced in self-protection to shoot Evelda Drumgo dead while she holds her baby. She shoots a mother – 'Evelda Drumgo bent over her baby in the road, her head tilted like that of a Cimabue Madonna, with the brains blown out...'

Harris's mother Polly is one of the very few people close to Thomas Harris ever to have spoken about him to reporters. Ten years ago, when she was 72 and the movie of *The Silence of the Lambs* was just out, she told the journalist Phoebe Hoban, he is 'the most gentle person I have ever known'.

In 1999, when she was 81 and *Hannibal* had been delivered but not yet published, she was quite garrulous to Caroline Graham. She called her son 'a gentle giant, a lovely boy who loves his mother very much'. She disclosed: 'I speak to Thomas every night. He is an only child and he runs everything past me. I've lived with this new book for ten years or more now. Thomas will ask me about certain passages and whether I think he's gone too far. I would never spoil the surprise, but I promise you this new book is the best one ever.'

She confirmed that she had indeed read *Hannibal*. 'I guess I was the first person who did. It kept me awake at night. And I'm his mother!' He still talks to her about his work, it seems. 'The subject matter is not altogether my cup of tea... But Thomas often asks my opinion about characters and things in his books. I tell him the truth. We are very close. Our relationship is deeper than mother and son, we are best friends. Of course, I have read everything he has written. And I am very proud of him.'

Consistently, her memories of his childhood are that he was a prodigious reader. 'Thomas was always an exceptional child. He was reading by the time he was three. He always had his nose in a book. He would say to me, "Mommy, I want to write when I grow up." And he said it with such conviction I never doubted him for a moment. He would read something and then go to the library and read more about a subject. He's still like that today. Everything you read in his books is fact.'

The other main source for these years, his uncle, Dr James Arch Coleman, an internal-medicine specialist, from Waco, Texas, confirms the picture of a studious boy. He says Harris 'grew up as an ordinary kid. He was quiet. He loved to read. He was as plain as an ordinary shoe.' There are plenty of such remarks about Harris.

Rich lies 16 miles north of the great blues town of Clarksdale, on Highway 61, the route up from Vicksburg to Memphis, immortalised by Bob Dylan: 'God said to Abraham, kill me a son...'

This is the Deep South, the heart of the Mississipi Delta, all flat fields and cotton plantations, crushing heat and shotgun shacks, so-called because you can shoot clear through them from the door. Apart from cotton, the main crops are catfish, soybeans, corn and rice. The area is still impoverished, with the highest proportion of house-holds without electricity or indoor plumbing anywhere in the United States. The per capita income averages $7,000 and blacks outnumber whites two to one.

The descendants of the cotton aristocracy live in a world of fine houses and country clubs. Naturally, the poorer whites in this society are hyperconscious of gentility – 'the uncertain gentility of the South', as it is called in *Hannibal*. Being clean, tidy, formally dressed and 'courteous' in speech matters. These are the Southern values at work in Clarice Starling when she first faces Lecter with her good bag and her cheap shoes, and her courtesy: 'My name is Clarice Starling. May I speak with you?' At the end of the interview, when Multiple Miggs flicks his semen over her, Lecter says: 'Discourtesy is unspeakably ugly to me.' In his closing letter, he promises that he has no plans to call on her: 'Be sure you extend me the same courtesy.' And, after the publication of *Hannibal*, when Harris came to describe, in a preface for a new edition of his novels, how he had to let his characters go their own ways – 'let Dr Lecter and Clarice Starling decide events according to their own nature' – he, too, put it like this: 'There is a certain amount of courtesy involved.'

In its day, Rich was 'the unofficial capital of the Cotton Kingdom in Northern Mississippi... the heart of the beast', as a blues historian puts it. Clarksdale is where 'Son' House, John Lee Hooker, Sam Cooke and Ike Turner were born and where Bessie Smith died in 1937, after a car accident. Nearly all the great bluesmen passed through here. The blues scholar Alan Lomax suggests that Clarksdale produced more blues artists than any other place in the world. Muddy Waters, born in Rolling Fork, was raised here and was working five miles south on Stoval's Plantation when Lomax made his marvellous Library of Congress recordings in 1941. The fearsome Parchman Penitentiary, sometime home to many of the great bluesmen, is 15 miles away on Highway 49. Clarksdale now boasts a Delta Blues Museum, until recently housed upstairs at the Carnegie

Public Library – the library whose staff Harris thanks in the Acknowledgements in *Hannibal*. 'The staff of Carnegie Public Library in Coahoma County, Mississippi, looked up things for years. Thank you.' But, aside from its role in the blues, Clarksdale is no great metropolis. Check it out on the Net and one of the first sites, after that of the town's Chamber of Commerce, reads: 'Clarksdale: It's a filthy town with no central planning whatsoever and drunk trouble-makers stand out in the middle of the road all the time.'

Rich itself is a farming settlement with very few people. A farmer there, Arthur Sanders, who has known Harris for a long time, says the place itself now has ten inhabitants and when Harris was growing up it would still have had only 20 or so. The immediate area contains no more than a few hundred people. The fields are huge and empty. Rich boasts one 'Stop' sign, but no traffic light.

What the South does have is its blood-soaked history, its battlegrounds, visited in due course by Harris in his fiction. 'What do you have when you come from a poor-white background? And from a place where Reconstruction didn't end until the 1950s...' we are asked, alongside Clarice Starling, in *Hannibal*. 'In what tradition do you find an example? That we whaled the piss out of them that first time at Bull Run? That

Great-granddaddy did right at Vicksburg, that a corner of Shiloh is forever Yazoo City?

'There is much honor and more sense in having succeeded with what was left, making something with the damned forty acres and a muddy mule, but you have to be able to see that. No one will tell you.'

It was here in Rich, in 1979, as he neared 40, that, according to his own account, Harris 'first encountered Hannibal Lecter, MD', when he returned home to the Delta 'owing to an illness in my family', that of his father. 'My neighbour in the village of Rich kindly gave me the use of a shotgun house in the centre of a vast cotton field, and there I worked, often at night... Sometimes at night I would leave the lights on in my little house and walk across the flat fields. When I looked back from a distance, the house looked like a boat at sea, and all around me the vast Delta night.' This is where he and his creation came together, in deep isolation.

From Rich, the young Thomas Harris went on to Clarksdale High School, the state school, and there he was not happy. In 1994, Harris wrote a wonderful article for a teen magazine called *Mouth2Mouth*, on the topic of 'An Ideal English Class Syllabus for 9th Graders'. It's a hymn to books and a denunciation of classrooms. Harris began by saying: 'A world odd enough to put me in charge of educating ninth-graders would also rotate end over end, I think, with the Western hemisphere forever dark... You must understand first that I wish I had never attended school, but had only been shown where the books are.' And he ended it with this advice: 'What older people think of as real life is no worse than the schoolyards we survive. By the time we reach the ninth grade, we've seen a lot of cruelty and brutish behaviour and wilful ignorance. It's hard to fashion a life that can withstand the weather. We can't do it without inner resources. School should help us develop them. Otherwise I recommend hooky.' It's plain he had a truly bad time in the schoolyard. It will also be remembered that Dr Lecter 'has extensive internal resources and can entertain himself for years at a time'.

In 1999, Meg Laughlin, a reporter from *Tulsa World*, talked to people in Rich who knew Harris as a boy. What they remembered was that he didn't fit in. 'He wasn't athletic at all, and even less interested in killing animals, and because of this, he didn't have friends his age. When sides were chosen for baseball at school, he was not picked. When it came to football, he knew not to approach the field. Mostly, he stayed at home and read.' If he did go out, it wasn't far. 'Sometimes as a child, Thomas Harris went to the

Yazoo Pass bridge with his cousins and shot at snakes and turtles with a .22. Sometimes, he played mumblety-peg with them throwing a knife in the ground, hoping it would stand up so he could win the game.'

He didn't have a lot of luck, it seems. Now Thomas Harris's enormously profitable works are registered as 'Copyright Yazoo Fabrications, Inc 1999'. None of these choices is random.

After they'd talked to Meg Laughlin, these Rich residents didn't want their names used. They were worried that Harris would mind. They were, one said, 'afraid he'll shun us, treat us the way he was treated when a child'. The Rich residents who didn't want their names used said too that 'Harris was describing his own childhood in *Black Sunday*, handing it over to his villain, setting it up as the motive for revenge and mass murder'.

Certainly *Black Sunday* is Harris's least sophisticated composition. Its villain, Michael Lander, grows up in rural South Carolina (Harris is careful never to name Mississippi in all his writing about the South). 'Michael's father is a minister and his mother is a power in the PTA. He is not a cute, appealing child. [At the age of eight] He thinks there is something terribly wrong with him. For as long as he can remember he has been filled with horrible feelings that he does not understand. He cannot yet identify rage and self-loathing. He has a constant picture of himself as a prissy little boy in short pants and he hates it.'

There is this key passage about the development of Michael Lander in *Black Sunday*. 'As a Southerner, Michael is deeply imprinted with the Code. A man fights when called on. A man is tough, straightforward, honourable and strong. He can play football, he loves to hunt, and he allows no nasty talk around the ladies, although he discusses them in lewd terms among his fellows.

'When you are a child, the Code without the equipment will kill you.'

At 14, Michael Lander has managed to get into the football game at last. 'The uniform makes him feel wonderfully anonymous.' This good time lasts just a week. His parents come to the game and haul him out in front of the other boys. 'Michael might have saved himself in that moment. He might have yelled in his mother's face.' He doesn't. Instead, he himself loses face irreparably and turns inside himself for ever.

At 15, he has constructed an appearance of mediocrity and affability. 'But in the blossoming of Michael Lander, part of him has stood off to the side, cold and watchful. It is the part of him that recognised the ignorance of the classroom, that constantly replays little vignettes of grade school making the new face wince, that flashes the picture of the unlovely little scholar in front of him in moments of stress, and can open under him a dread void when his new image is threatened.

'The little scholar stands at the head of a legion of hate and he knows the answer every time, and his creed is God Damn You All... At fifteen Lander functions very well. A trained observer might notice a few things about him that hint at his feelings, but these in themselves are not suspicious. He cannot bear personal competition. He has never experienced the gradients of controlled aggression that allow most of us to survive. He cannot even endure board games... Emotionally, for him there is no middle ground between a pleasant, uncompetitive atmosphere and total war to the death with the corpse defiled and burned. So he has no outlet. And he has swallowed his poison longer than most could have done.'

It would be too crude to say that this 'little scholar' was Thomas Harris, although by his mother's own account he was a little scholar. But here, at any rate, is the first stirring of the fearful intimacy with savage and revengeful fantasy that makes a first encounter with *Red Dragon* and *The Silence of the Lambs* so shaking. All social accounts of Thomas Harris emphasise his gentleness and, yes, his courtesy. Every reader of his books knows there is more to him. As Lecter dismisses Clarice after their third meeting, in which she has begun to tell him about her childhood, he says: 'Next time you'll tell me two things. What happened with the horse is one. The other thing I wonder is... how do you manage your rage?' Dr Lecter is not interested in the horse.

Thomas Harris left Clarksdale High School and moved to live with his aunt in Cleveland, Mississippi, 35 miles south of Clarksdale on Highway 61, the home town of Delta State University. Cleveland is where his mother Polly now lives too, having moved out of Rich after husband's death.

At Cleveland High School, Harris prospered. He sang in the chorus and had a part in the school play. He became friends with a boy called Stanley Gaines who had a 1956 red Ford convertible and they drove around listening to Elvis and going to the local drive-in burger joints. 'Gaines always had a girlfriend; Harris didn't.' Gaines later became the chief executive of a Mississippi oil company.

Harris didn't go to Delta State or the University of Mississippi, 'Ole Miss', in Oxford, the bastion of the Old South. Perhaps this was because of the racial trouble brewing there at the time. In 1962 there were ugly riots when the first black student, James Meredith, enrolled. Troops were called in and two men died. Or perhaps Harris just knew that he had to leave Mississippi. 'He just wanted to go off to Texas there,' says one of his Rich neighbours.

So Harris went to Baylor University in Texas, a long way west, to major in English. There's a freshman picture of him there in 1961. He's lean, bespectacled, neatly dressed and coiffed, with a fixed smile, looking off a little to the side. Baylor is a religious university, to put it mildly. Actually, it's the largest Baptist university in the world, founded in 1845, occupying a 432-acre campus, on the banks of the Brazos River, in Waco. To some it's known as 'Thee University'.

Baylor is affiliated to the Baptist General Convention of Texas and its motto, believe it or not, is *'Pro Ecclesia, Pro Texana'*. The official literature states that this 'remains the foundation of its mission'. There are currently around 13,000 students and it offers a four-year undergraduate course. 'Baylor's strong core curriculum is based on the liberal arts, crosses all majors, and emphasises analytical skills and ethical practices', the prospectus promises. In the 1980s and early 1990s, the control of Baylor was fiercely contested between moderate and fundamentalist Baptists, the latter wanting to convert it into something like a straightforward Bible college. Some 90 per cent of its students are Christian. They have been known to wear T-shirts saying things like 'Our God is Awesome', or 'The Lord's Gym – No Pain, No Gain'. Drinking and dancing are, in theory at least, not allowed on campus. 'Parents think of Baylor as a safe place', wrote one commentator in 1994. 'Even the most fundamentalist parents are convinced their kids won't come home pregnant, gay, perverted, un-Christian, un-American, anti-Bible...' In the 1990s, the models in the life-drawing classes on campus were compelled by the administration to wear swimsuits. The religious life of Bible Belt America is like no other. How to put this tactfully? It's both omnipresent and strikingly stupid. That's part of the background to Harris's work, reaching a strange flowering in the sustained blasphemies of *Hannibal*.

When Harris went to Baylor in the early 1960s, it was probably no more advanced than it is now, less if anything. These days he might just be Baylor's most famous graduate. But the author of Dr Lecter – he who collects church collapses, recreationally – is not, we may guess, the university's favourite son. Nor is Harris piously attached to his alma mater. He's returned to Texas, to Baptists in general and to Baylor in particular several times, in fiction at least. In the first of Dr Lecter's remarkable letters, towards the end of *Red*

Dragon, there is this: 'You may have noticed in the paper yesterday, God dropped a church roof on thirty-four of His worshippers in Texas Wednesday night – just as they were grovelling through a hymn. Don't you think that felt good? Thirty-four.' There's Sammie, in *The Silence of the Lambs*, with his great poem not so dissimilar to the Baylor T-shirts:

I WAN TOO GO TO JESA

I WAN TOO GO WIV CRIEZ

I CAN GO WIV JESA

EF I AC RELL NIZE

Lecter tells Clarice: 'Sammie put his mother's head in the collection plate at the Highway Baptist Church in Trune. They were singing "Give of Your Best to the Master" and it was the nicest thing he had.'

There are specific hits at Baylor too. In *Hannibal*, Mason Verger's father, Molson Verger, the meatpacking mogul who fought the Humane Slaughter Act and managed to keep facebranding legal, leaves a will in which, 'In the absence of an heir, the sole beneficiary shall be the Southern Baptist Convention with specific clauses concerning Baylor University at Waco, Texas.'

And Mason Verger brings in, for psychiatric insight into Hannibal Lecter, Dr Doemling, 'head of the psychology department at Baylor University' where he holds the 'Verger Chair'. Dr Doemling, 'a dry person, extremely clean but flaking, with a dry comb-over on his spotted scalp and a Phi Beta Kappa key on his watch chain', gives a little lecture about the relationship between Hannibal and Clarice, complete with slides. 'This is a classic example of what I have termed in my published work avunculism – it's beginning to be referred to broadly in the professional literature as Doemling's avunculism. Possibly it will be included in the next Diagnostic and Statistical Manual.'

Unfortunately, Barney, the warder who looked after Lecter, is present and he remembers Dr Doemling. 'I was in charge of the ward when you tried to talk to Dr Lecter, a lot of people tried it, but you're the one who left crying as I recall. Then he reviewed your book in the *American Journal of Psychiatry*. I couldn't blame you if the review made you cry.' So Thomas Harris has not entirely left Baylor behind him.

While at Baylor Harris had begun working nights on the *Waco News Tribune* on crime stories and eventually got a full-time job there as a crime reporter. His editor, Bob Sadler, remembered that he never went for the obvious, 'he picked up small details and nuances that made people come alive'. A fellow student-reporter, Dallas Lee, remembered: 'He was game to look into anything. He was fascinated with gathering facts, information and angles.' Lee has a story about Harris going into Mexico to report on a child-prostitution ring: 'There was murder and intrigue and this terrible thing involving children. He had an appetite to examine the horrors of existence... and a curiosity to know about these things.' When his former publisher in Britain, Helen Fraser, asked him if there had been any real-life inspiration for Hannibal Lecter, Harris mentioned a doctor he had met in a Mexican jail who had murdered several people.

At about this time, it appears, Harris also contributed to such fantasy magazines as *True* and *Argosy*. The reporting and the fantasy hadn't yet melded perhaps.

Harris graduated in 1964. In his last year as an undergraduate, he had married a fellow-student, Harriet, and they had a daughter, Anne. When Harris eventually left Waco, his wife remained behind and they were divorced while his daughter was still a small child. Harris travelled rough in Europe for a while. He didn't go back to live in the South. From 1968 to 1974, he worked at Associated Press in New York, at their offices in Rockefeller Plaza, first as a general reporter and then as a night editor.

A colleague there, Nick Pileggi, remembered: 'We all covered inordinate amounts of crime... Liquor-store robberies, murders. Really grungy stuff. I can't tell you how low we were on AP's talent scale. They thought of us as the garbage pail. Tom was this classic old boy and he'd be out on assignment with all these New York guys saying "dese, dem and dose".' Another colleague remembered him as an unusually precise editor. 'Harris spent hours poring over copy, marking it with a pen, taking more time with each article than any of the other editors.'

In 1973 Harris, now in his early thirties, and two other AP reporters, Sam Maull and Dick Riley, came up with the idea of writing a thriller together. The massacre at Lod (Tel Aviv) airport, by PLO-trained Japanese terrorists, had happened in May 1972: 23 were killed, 76 wounded, by the three gunmen. The PLO attack at the Munich Olympics had followed in September.

The trio decided to combine these events into an attack by a non-Palestinian terrorist on a major sporting event in the States: *Black Sunday*. They sold the book to Putnam and split the advance. It seems they did begin to write it together too but Harris soon bought out his co-authors and took over. *Black Sunday* was published in 1975; and the film appeared quickly in 1977. This success freed Harris from journalism: Freddy Lounds was the result in his second book. But then, journalists do know about journalism, if nothing else.

Four: Black Sunday

There's a lot of Thomas Harris in *Black Sunday* but not all his talent. It's an efficient thriller, not much more. The reviews were positive but modest, mostly just stating that it worked well enough as a page-turner: 'a racing read' (*The Times*), 'inescapably readable thriller' (*The Guardian*), 'a riveting read' (*The Daily Mail*).

The subject is international terrorism, Black September versus the Israeli secret services, and though it's well enough handled, this is not a theme with any profound personal resonance for Harris. Nor is it one with much in-built longevity. *Black Sunday* is of its time and no more. The book opens with an Israeli raid on the headquarters of Black September in Beirut, an action-opening of the kind Harris later used in *Hannibal*. Among the survivors is Dahlia Iyad, a committed Palestinian terrorist. She is developing a weapon, a suicide-bomber: Michael Lander, an American, a former helicopter pilot and Vietnam POW, now quite mad, who wants to kill as many people as possible in one deadly conflagration.

Lander works as the pilot of a blimp, used for filming aerial views of sports events. He has dreamed up a form of gigantic Claymore mine to be suspended beneath the blimp, shaped like the stadium in miniature and studded with thousands of lethal darts, to kill all the spectators at the New Orleans Super Bowl at once, including, he hopes, his former wife and the American President. (Sam Maull said that 'using the Goodyear blimp as the delivery vehicle for the explosives was Tom's idea', incidentally.)

The rest of the book is a Will he? Won't he? Black September get the plastic explosives that Lander needs to him – but in doing so they are detected and pursued by Mossad operatives. David Kabakov and Robert Moshevsky, Mossad's finest, fly to America to try to hunt down the Palestinians, their creature and the unexploded bomb, being obstructed rather than assisted by the American secret service. Meanwhile, Dahlia Iyad and her fellow terrorist Muhammad Fasil try to nurse the unstable Lander along to the fulfilment of his mission. En route, they try to bump off the Israelis too. The contest remains undecided until the last second – and the outcome is, a little surprisingly for the genre, not entirely happy. Harris never lets anybody get away without damage.

Harris appears to have used the book to learn how

to make a thriller work. It is already extremely deftly organised and weaves together multiple threads of the hunters and the hunted with considerable skill. But the book's basic premise – Israelis good, Palestinians, in fact Arabs, bad – is none too subtle.

The troika of authors picked up their idea from the news. Maull has said that the opening scene was taken quite straightforwardly from the front page of the *New York Times*. In the book, Michael Lander gets the idea for his plot off the news too. Lander is already on the lookout for a source of plastic explosive when, in a Cincinnati motel, he sees footage of the attack on television: 'Cut to Munich. The horror at the Olympic village. The helicopter at the airport. Muffled gunfire inside it as the Israeli athletes were shot. The embassy at Khartoum where the American and Belgian diplomats were slain. Al Fatah leader Yasser Arafat denying responsibility.'

At this stage, Lander knows no Arabs. He has no interest in the cause. He just wants to kill as many people as he can in one go – or, to put it another way, he's not planning to be a serial killer, he wants to be a mass-murderer. His connection with Palestinian terrorists is quite as opportunistic as the plotting of these three journalists turned thriller-writer.

The novel's debts to recent events are smartly

acknowledged in the opening scene. Muhammad Fasil, who gets the plastic explosives to Lander, is described as 'ordnance expert and architect of the attack on the Olympic Village at Munich'. Dahlia Iyad is even more boldly linked to recent events. 'Dahlia had helped to train the three Japanese terrorists who struck at Lod Airport in Tel Aviv, slaying at random. Originally there had been four Japanese terrorists. One lost his nerve in training, and, with the other three watching, Dahlia blew his head off with a Schmeisser machine pistol.'

Any astute journalist on the lookout for the pretext for a political thriller in the mid–1970s might have come up with the idea of Palestinian terrorism on the loose in the United States, but once Harris had taken over from his collaborators the book did begin to acquire an individual voice.

There are still plenty of clunky thriller-writing-by-numbers sentences here, including the first: 'Night fell as the airport taxi rattled along the six miles of coastal road into Beirut.' But there are, too, some phrases reaching towards the oracular manner of Harris's later books. 'Black September lives within Al Fatah as desire lives in the body,' we are told. That's Harris, in embryo.

Moreover, Michael Lander is the first of Harris's 'monsters', decisively referred to as such, always. Dahlia, it is said, 'learned' him well. 'Dahlia had it from the monster's mouth.' But Muhammed Fasil is also baldly given the title of monster: 'Fasil was living proof that physiognomy is a false science. He was slim and fairly good-looking. He was a monster.' Later, in the form of Francis Dolarhyde and Jame Gumb, Harris builds horror by exploring the way that a serial killer feeds off his fantasies and progresses along a path of evil, each crime developing on its predecessors. Here, Lander plans just the one devastating enormity. The tension builds only on the question of whether or not he will succeed. It's not a novel that much rewards rereading or that lives in the memory vividly, as Harris's hypnotic later works do. Already, however, Harris shows some of his alarming empathy with the nature of murderous fantasy. The possible similarity between some of Lander's boyhood and moments in Harris's has already been described. Harris, of course, if he ever harboured fantasies of revenge, made art of them. Lander plans only death.

The moment which finally turns Lander into the monster – when he finds his wife, Margaret, in bed with her lover – is described as the death of his will. 'He believed that it passed out through his mouth and nose in a thin smoke riding on a sigh.'

Now, he is no longer fully a man. 'The remains of the man Lander would feel some pain, would jerk galvanically like frog's legs in a skillet, would cry out for relief. But he would never again sink his teeth into the pumping heart of rage. Rage would never again cut out his heart and rub it pumping in his face.

'What was left could live with rage because it was made in rage and rage was its element and it thrived there as a mammal thrives in air.'

Lander still functions, though. 'The man functioned perfectly because the child needed him, needed his quick brain and clever fingers. To find its own relief. By killing and killing and killing and killing. And dying.' It's an early example of Harris making his prose embody the madness of the thoughts, a skill he will later refine.

Then Lander has his 'epiphany' about what he will do, how he can kill the most. 'Sometimes, as he lay awake, the upturned faces of the crowd filled his midnight ceiling, mouths open, shifting like a field of flowers in the wind. Many of the faces became Margaret's. Then the great fireball lifted off the heat of his face and rose to them, swirling like the Crab nebula, searing them to charcoal, soothing him to sleep.' (The stars are always important in Harris, as are the elements – Lecter is to tell Clarice that we are 'elaborations of carbon'.)

The pulsing, visionary tone of this – Harris writes

already as if he knows the inside of these minds – is uncommon. But *Black Sunday* still lacks the deep contextualising, the depth of secondary characterisation and the awareness of universal struggle that makes the later books so unsettling. The later books present a fiercely coherent view of life as we all must endure it. *Black Sunday* merely presents Arab fanatics hooking up with a raging lunatic.

Yet there's a glimpse of what is to come. The Israeli agent, Kabakov, was possibly modelled on real Israeli commandos such as Meir Dagan. However, more importantly, just as Lander is Harris's first monster, Kabakov is the first, not yet fully developed, example of the man-hunter in Harris's fiction, the force for order who is uneasy about what it is in his own nature that makes him good at his job. There's a passage about this in which Harris can almost be seen intuiting his future theme. Kabakov remembers stopping his jeep once, years ago, on a mountainside near Tiberias in Galilee. He watches a flock of sheep grazing above him.

A sense of aloneness pressed around him and made him aware of the shape and position of his body in these great tilted spaces. And then he saw an eagle, high, riding a thermal, wingtip feathers splayed like fingers, slipping sideways over the mountain's face, his shadow slipping fast over the rocks. The eagle was not hunting sheep, for it was winter and there were no lambs among them, but it was above the sheep and they saw it and baaed among themselves. Kabakov became dizzy watching the bird, his horizontal reference distorted by the mountain slope. He found himself holding on to the jeep for balance.

And then he realised that he loved the eagle better than the sheep and that he always would and that, because he did, because it was in him to do it, he could never be perfect in the sight of God.

Kabakov was glad that he would never have any real power.

This baroque passage clearly presages the 'silence of the lambs' story told by Clarice Starling. It shows Harris beginning to develop the extraordinarily vigorous natural imagery and observation that drives his subsequent books and embodies his sense of the pitilessness of the struggle for life. In his world, predation is the norm, in both animals and humans. His murderers are big predators, and predating on them is the biggest of them all, Dr Lecter. He hunts the other hunters down and eats them up. Nor is Harris's sense of this carnivorous world conveyed just in imagery: animals are actually there in his books, to an extent no other thriller writer has ever rivalled. The pigs and the moray eel in *Hannibal* may seem at first sight strangely cumbersome and roundabout devices, peculiarly elaborate means of vengeance. But they have their rationale. And anyway you might say as much of the punishments in Dante.

Harris has made the theme of the universal struggle for life explicit once, at the end of *Red Dragon* – perhaps an artistic mistake. Will Graham visits Shiloh, the battleground where so many died in April 1862. He sees a broken-backed chicken snake in the road. He picks it up by its tail and cracks it like a whip.

> Its brains zinged into the pond. A bream rose to them.
>
> He had thought Shiloh haunted, its beauty sinister like flags.
>
> Now, drifting between memory and narcotic sleep, he saw that Shiloh was not sinister; it was indifferent. Beautiful Shiloh could witness anything. Its unforgivable beauty simply underscored the indifference of nature, the Green Machine. The loveliness of Shiloh mocked our plight... In the Green Machine there is no mercy; *we* make mercy, manufacture it in the parts that have overgrown our basic reptile brain.
>
> There is no murder. We make murder, and it matters only to us.

Throughout Harris's books, the Green Machine (poor

phrase) is ferociously at work, first at the level of metaphor and then, in the strange fruition of Hannibal, as a kind of actuality.

In *Black Sunday*, the incidence of the imagery is relatively sparse. Lander is a snake. 'His mind was as cool as snake's blood.' The observant Dahlia sees this snake in him from the start. 'She was apprehensive, but not so much as before their first meeting – then she had felt that she was in the room with a snake she could not see. After she came to live with him, she separated the deadly part of Michael Lander from the rest of him. When she was with him now, she felt that they were both in a room with a snake, and she could tell where it was, and whether it was sleeping.' But Harris's great snake was still to come: Hannibal Lecter.

Five: Serial Killers and Red Dragon

Thomas Harris celebrated the sale of *Black Sunday* with a champagne dinner at La Petite Ferme with a friend from Associated Press, Tom Goldstein. Then he gave up journalism and came up with *Red Dragon*. Or, to put it another way, he took the time to become an entirely different kind of writer. *Black Sunday* is gripping enough. It's not frightening. *Red Dragon*, published six years later, is terrifying. There'd been nothing quite like it before. It opened up new possibilities in crime fiction for dozens of writers following in Harris's wake.

Now that serial-killer fiction has become such a staple, indeed a humdrum recourse for the talentless, it's easy to forget what a shock *Red Dragon* gave its first readers and maybe even its writer too. Lanford Wilson, a neighbour and friend, once told a reporter that Harris himself had been alarmed by what he had produced. 'He said when *Red Dragon* came out in hardback, he took it down to the beach and started to read it, and was horrified that he had written it. Because of the madness and violence. He said, "My God, where did that come from?" He horrified himself.'

There are several new departures for crime fiction in *Red Dragon*. There is the arrival in the world of Dr Hannibal Lecter, for one. For another, there is the first use in fiction of the 'profiling' work of the FBI's Behavioral Science Unit in Quantico, with all that implied for the way a narrative could be structured and a murderer pursued. Then there is the presentation of a fully-fledged serial killer as villain. Although many villains before had committed multiple murder (the first of Patricia Highsmith's Ripley stories, *The Talented Mr Ripley*, appeared in 1956), none before had been so closely modelled on what was known about real murderers driven by fantasy to kill again and again. Nor had any previous crime book presented a crime scene with such detailed horror as that uncovered at the start of *Red Dragon*. Nor had the thought-processes of a monster been made so intimately plausible to the reader as they are in the scenes in which Dolarhyde is taken over by the Dragon.

Although five or six years seems a long time to spend writing a thriller, Harris had actually identified a new trend extremely fast. No sooner had detectives begun interviewing killers in an attempt to understand their motivation, than Harris had digested their work and turned it into fiction.

In the late 1970s, Harris carefully studied the work of Robert Ressler and John Douglas at the Behavioral Science Unit at Quantico. It will be remembered that at this time Ressler had only just invented the term 'serial killer'. John Douglas joined the unit of nine agents in June 1977. Ressler's first interview with a convicted killer, for the purposes of 'research', wasn't until the spring of 1978, when he went to see Sirhan Sirhan, the paranoid schizophrenic who assassinated Robert F. Kennedy.

In his memoir *Mindhunter,* Douglas says it was he who first had the idea of trying to learn from actual meetings with convicted killers. One day early in 1978, he and Ressler together had been teaching a 'road school' to the local police department. 'Right from the beginning, I felt uncomfortable about what amounted to teaching from "hearsay". Most of the instructors – myself prime among them – had no direct experience with the vast majority of the cases they taught. In that way, it was very much like a college course in criminology where, in most cases, the professor has never been out in the streets experiencing the kind of things he's talking about.'

For his part, in *Whoever Fights Monsters*, Ressler seems to contradict this when he says, 'in early 1978, I was to go to northern California to teach at a road school, and I saw a window of opportunity'. Whichever. According to Ressler, he only brought Douglas, 'a young, flamboyant agent whom I had earlier championed into the BSU', into the project after he had already conducted the first few interviews with another agent, John Conway.

At any rate, Douglas says, 'By the time Ressler and I had done ten or 12 prison interviews, it was clear to any reasonably intelligent observer that we were on to something. For the first time, we were able to correlate what was going on in an offender's mind with the evidence he left at a crime scene.'

They brought in Dr Ann Burgess, a professor of psychiatric mental-health nursing at the University of Pennsylvania School of Nursing. She got a $400,000 grant from the National Institute for Justice to further the research – and developed a 'fifty-seven page instrument to be filled out for each interview'. ('Oh, Officer Starling, do you think you can dissect me with this blunt little tool?' says Lecter, sending Clarice's questionnaire back, in the opening scene of *The Silence of the Lambs*.) By 1983 – after the publication of *Red Dragon* – they had completed a detailed study of 36 individuals. Only in 1988 did Burgess, Douglas and Ressler eventually publish the standard manual: *Sexual Homicide: Patterns and Motives*.

One of the main distinctions this textbook proposes is between 'organised' and 'disorganised' killers. It offers lists of the different characteristics of each type of murderer and the different crime scenes they leave. (Organised: Body hidden, weapon/evidence absent, transports victim or body... Disorganised: Body left in view, evidence/weapon often present, body left at death scene... etc.) This concept is also derided by Lecter, who says that 'most psychology is puerile, Officer Starling, and that practised in Behavioral Science is on a level with phrenology... Organised and disorganised – a real bottom-feeder thought of that.'

Harris picked up on the work of the Behavioral Science Unit at a very early stage – his first visit seems to have been as early as 1978 – and used it extensively but not with unequivocal admiration. Did Ressler and Douglas realise that he was studying them as much as their work? Perhaps not. It seems that until Harris became famous they merely found him self-effacing.

Douglas: 'Harris was a real quiet guy, very studious, an academic type. He wouldn't be the life of the party... He'd observe the instruction, and then he'd sit in the office and discuss in a little more depth some of the cases.'

Ressler: 'Harris was like a sponge, saying little but absorbing everything. We also discussed my already lengthy series of prison interviews, and I told him that lately we had been bringing various psychiatrists and other mental-health experts into the Bureau for consultation. Later, Tom Harris fused the idea of prison interviews with reaching out to psychiatrists and used that in his novel *Red Dragon*, where the FBI agent turns for help to the now-celebrated character of Hannibal Lecter, the psychiatrist and incarcerated serial killer who helps solve the mystery. The character and plot are entirely Harris's, of course, but I am proud to have provided some facts on which his fertile imagination could work.'

Grotesquely, the pair have both sold many books on the basis of being the 'real' Jack Crawford. Douglas ends *Mindhunter* by saying: 'Not too long ago, I was invited to speak before the New York chapter of the Mystery Writers of America... In fact, ever since Thomas Harris and *The Silence of the Lambs*, writers and newspeople and film-makers have been coming to us for the "real story".'

Ressler, more sharply, complains at the end of *Whoever Fights Monsters* that the FBI itself has jumped on to the bandwagon, allowing Quantico to be used as a set for the film of *The Silence of the Lambs* and for personnel to appear in cameo roles. 'New applicants to the BSU are taking Jodie Foster's character as a role model; they, too, want to be super-sleuths.' This was written before Clarice had gone to the bad in *Hannibal* – but perhaps it would make no difference anyway. Undeterred, the FBI launched a recruiting drive for women agents on the back of the film of *Hannibal*.

Ressler: 'As a society, we seem to be flying too close to the flame, looking for stimulation – we are bored audiences more attuned to fantasy than to reality, in danger of falling completely into the abyss about which Nietzsche warned us.'

His title alludes to a saying from *Thus Spake Zarathustra*: 'Whoever fights monsters should see to it that in the process he does not become a monster. And when you look into any abyss, the abyss also looks into you.' It's a thoroughly Harrisian thought. In the preface to the omnibus edition, Harris gives his account of how he 'encountered Hannibal Lecter, MD'. Harris always speaks of his characters this way, never of having made them up. He insists: 'You must understand that when you are writing a novel you are not making anything up. It's all there and you just have to find it.' More specifically: 'To write a novel, you begin with what you can see and then you add what came before and what came after.'

He was back home in Rich at the time of his father's final illness, working at night. He could see, he says, 'the investigator Will Graham in the home of the victim family, in the house where they all died, watching the dead family's home movies. I pushed to find out, to see what came before and what came after. I went through the home, the crime scene, in the dark with Will and could see no more and no less than he could see.'

Here, then, is the origin of the extraordinarily powerful scene in Chapter 2 of *Red Dragon* in which Will Graham walks around the house where a whole family has been murdered and guesses what has happened there. The investigator and the novelist are both playing the same part, both seeing the same scene, both trying to understand what must have come before and what might come after. 'Graham wondered if he had lit a candle. The flickering light would simulate expression on their faces. No candle was found. Maybe he would think to do that next time...' Graham intuits the movements of the madman's mind and sees what might come next. 'This first small bond to the killer itched and stung like a leech.' Then he also grasps what came before: 'You took off your gloves, didn't you? The powder came out of a rubber glove as you pulled it off to touch her, DIDN'T IT, YOU SON OF A BITCH.' Graham is reading the crime scene.

In his account of the creation of Lecter, Harris continues: 'Will Graham had to ask somebody, he needed some help and he knew it', as ever maintaining the fiction that the characters act independently of his will. 'He knew where he had to go, long before he let himself think about it. I knew Graham had been severely damaged in a previous case. I knew he was terribly reluctant to consult the best source he had. At this time, I myself was accruing painful memories every day and in my evening's work I felt for Graham.'

It's a rare acknowledgement of where some of the pain that so imbues his novels came from, a kinship acknowledged. It's also a telling choice of words: to describe experience as 'accruing painful memories every day' reveals much about his understanding of what makes up our lives in time, of which way we face, of what we're made.

One of the impressive achievements of *Red Dragon* is how late it all starts. Few other writers, having dreamed up Hannibal Lecter, would have had the discipline to introduce him at the point when his story seems to have ended and he has already spent three years in prison. Partly, this is a method – a highly successful method – of establishing him as already legendary. Partly, it is to make Lecter purely a mind, to make him another reader, like us, immobilised, interpreting rather than acting. But it reflects, too, the whole tone of the book in which so much pain has already been inflicted – so many memories already been accrued, in that curious phrase. There are scars, those physical memories of injury, all around in *Red Dragon*. First there is the scar that is Dolarhyde's upper lip. There's that 'looping scar' inscribed on Will Graham by Hannibal Lecter. And, on the morning after Dolarhyde's night with Reba McClane, there is this ominous comparison: 'Almost blind to his true feelings, no more able to express them than a scar can blush, Dolarhyde did not know what had happened to him, or why.'

None of these echoing words and images are

accidental in Harris, so careful is his control. Later, in *The Silence of the Lambs*, Lecter will say of Jack Crawford that he is wise: 'His face is all scars if you know how to look. Well, possibly there's room for a few more.'

Red Dragon opens with Jack Crawford persuading Will Graham to come out of retirement, to leave his family and take on a new case. A madman has killed two entire families in their homes. Crawford promises that the already badly damaged Graham 'won't have to fight'. He's wrong.

Graham visits the most recent crime scene, the house of the Leeds family, and comprehends what happened there. The madman arranged the corpses of the children in a row, so that they could watch 'a performance starring the madman and the body of Mrs Leeds, beside Mr Leeds in the bed'. Graham suddenly realises where the killer may have left a fingerprint, on the eye of one of the victims.

After a second visit to the house, Graham learns more about the Leeds family. He reads a diary, he watches them on a home video. Realising he is not getting anywhere, he resolves to go to see Dr Lecter. Lecter reads the case-notes and suggests that the killer, who smashes the mirrors and inserts the shards into his victims, is 'a very shy boy' and possibly disfigured.

Then comes a shock. We are introduced without ambiguity to the killer. Francis Dolarhyde is seen first at work, at a film laboratory, Gateway, then at home, where he watches the movie he has made of the murder. We are told that he plans many such films and that he selects the victims from their home movies. 'Families were mailing their applications to him every day.' From this point on, it is evident that this is a novel not of teasing detection but of dread.

Graham goes to the first crime scene and again puts himself in the murderer's place, enabling him to discover the Red Dragon character that Dolarhyde incised on a tree.

Back to Dolarhyde and into his madness. He reads the 'great ledger' he has compiled devoted to the Dragon. 'Fastened in the margins, ragged bites of scalp trailed their tails of hair like comets pressed in God's scrapbook.' He contemplates Lecter.

Lecter, he believes, 'alone among all men might have the sensitivity and experience to understand the glory, the majesty of Dolarhyde's Becoming.

'Dolarhyde felt that Lecter knew the unreality of the people who die to help you in these things – understood that they are not flesh, but light and air and colour and quick sounds, quickly ended when you change them. Like balloons of colour bursting. That they are more important for the changing, more important than the lives they scrabble after, pleading.

'Dolarhyde bore screams as a sculptor bears dust from the beaten stone.'

Dolarhyde writes to Lecter, as 'Avid Fan'. Although the letter is found and shown to Crawford, Lecter manages to respond with a small ad in the *National Tattler* in code. It tells Dolarhyde where Graham lives and suggests he kill him and his family. Graham loses his family's trust.

Crawford attempts to lure the murderer out with a proactive phoney article in the *Tattler*. The result of that is the murder of the reporter, Lounds. Now it is just Graham against the Dragon. The narrative switches back to give Dolarhyde's story, his deformity, his abandonment, his growing fantasy life, his reconstructive surgery, his bodybuilding, his use of his grandmother's teeth – and his discovery of a fantasy identity in Blake's watercolour of the Great Red Dragon.

Then Dolarhyde meets, at work, the blind Reba McClane, one of Harris's courageous women. When he finds that she will accept him as he is, he tries to pull back from the fantasy. He confronts the Dragon, in an extraordinary dialogue. In an attempt to master the Dragon, he goes to the Brooklyn Museum to eat the

Blake watercolour (Harris enjoys these outrages on reality, as when later Hannibal claims the painter Balthus as his cousin). Dolarhyde believes he can now protect Reba McClane from the Dragon.

But Will Graham has guessed how the victims are being selected. He knows the killer has seen their home movies and must work in a film lab. The FBI are waiting for Dolarhyde at Gateway. The Dragon erupts. He convincingly fakes his death in a fire and escapes, returning later to attack Graham and his family at home, as Lecter suggested. Graham is again badly cut. The Dragon is eventually killed not by the FBI but by Graham's wife. As she shoots him, he gasps 'Muhner'.

In hospital, Graham drifts away into a dream about his visit to the Civil War battleground, Shiloh. He realises that murder is human.

Graham knew too well that he contained all the elements to make murder; perhaps mercy too.

He understood murder uncomfortably well though.

He wondered if, in the great body of humankind, in the minds of men set on civilisation, the vicious urges we control in ourselves and the dark instinctive knowledge of those urges function like the crippled virus the body arms against.

He wondered if old, awful urges are the virus that makes vaccine.

It's an uncharacteristically awkward, opaque and actually badly written paragraph for Harris. It is perhaps meant as a rationale for the novel, as much as for Graham's insight into murder. It's as if Harris is saying 'the old, awful urges' are worth thinking about as part of the price of civilisation – and therefore his kind of crime novel deserves consideration as a serious form of literature. It's a pity he felt the need to do this within the body of the text. The Blakean frontispiece and the impressive epigraph from the early criminologist Bertillon, followed by the quotations from *Songs of Innocence* and *Songs of Experience*, locate the book within the literary tradition much more effectively. As indeed does the great distinction – the clarity, musicality and authority – of the prose. In any case, it is obvious to any reader that much more is going on in *Red Dragon* than is usual in a thriller.

Yes, Harris's thrillers feature deranged serial killers and they do so more powerfully than any previous crime fiction, but they are not exclusively or even primarily about them. How moved or engaged could we be if they were? They are so gripping – gripping on multiple rereadings too – because, beneath the superb engineering of the thriller, there is an absolutely clear and savage view of the conditions of life for us all. We all are held by our past; we all seek to change. We all desire; we all fear. The books use their genre to draw a dramatic picture. Only the most cloddish adherent of literature as a delegation from an interest-group could think that because the books are melodramatic they have no bearing on ordinary life. Literature is imaginative, not representative.

Take a look. The books are full of piercing observations about such common feelings as the experience of ageing. When Harris was completing *Red Dragon*, his first real book, he was coming up for 40. That's one of the things the novel is about. Harris is a writer who always knows how old his characters are and what it means for them. 'Graham was nearly 40 and just beginning to feel the tug of the way the world was then; it was a sea anchor streamed behind him in heavy weather.' Later, it is said: 'It seemed to Graham that he had learned nothing in 40 years; he had just gotten tired.'

Francis Dolarhyde (born in 1938) is 42 at the time *Red Dragon* takes place. It's already been noted that 'he had known since the age of nine that essentially he was alone and that he would always be alone, a conclusion more common to the forties.' His insanity has been triggered two years earlier.

'One small event, which occurs to everybody, told the seed in his skull it was Time: standing by a north window, examining some film, he noticed ageing in his hands. It was as though his hands, holding the film, had suddenly appeared before him and he saw in that good north light that the skin had slackened over the bones and tendons and his hands were creased in diamonds as small as lizard scales.' (Does Dolarhyde mean dolour hide, the pain of being in one's skin?) A week later he comes upon the Blake painting: 'The Great Red Dragon and the Woman Clothed with the Sun'. The dragon has no scales.

Lecter – perhaps also born in 1938? – is 41 at the time of *Red Dragon*. Frederick Chilton comes upon him reading an actuarial chart on which he has written his age. '"And what do you have here?" Chilton asked. "Time," Dr Lecter said.' Thus the three main characters are close in age, close in age too to their author. Harris has effaced himself from his book, that superbly constructed machine. But he is more truly there in his handiwork than he is anywhere else. The Harris of report – in Sag Harbor and Miami, cooking, jolly, shy, polite – is not of equivalent interest.

Then see, too, how Harris has placed his most minor characters in the same terminal context in which the primary struggle is being waged. It's one of the ways in which Harris has made his novels so tremendously energised as a view of the whole human condition.

One memorable example. In *Red Dragon*, Will Graham, just back from visiting the house where the Leeds family died, steps into a lift with a couple of unnamed businessmen, wearing name-tags printed 'Hi!':

They held on to the rail and looked over the lobby as they ascended.

'Looka yonder by the desk – that's Wilma and them just coming in,' the larger one said. 'Goddam, I'd love to tear off a piece of that.'

'Fuck her till her nose bleeds,' the other one said.

Fear and rut, and anger at the fear.

'Say, do you know why a woman has legs?'

'Why?'

'So she won't leave a trail like a snail.'

The elevator doors opened.

'Is this it? This is it,' the larger one said. He lurched against the facing as he got off.

'This is the blind leading the blind,' the other one said.

The scene is brutal; the rhythm, though, is formal, almost Flaubertian. It has the effect of making the monstrous crimes seem not so removed from common ugliness.

Notice, too, the growing pressure of the animal imagery on the narrative. Harris, we can guess if we want to, likes animals and has lived close to them. In one of his publicity pictures, he poses with a spaniel, his arm around it, its leg across his as if reciprocating. In his preface about the writing of the three Hannibal books, he mentions that, working in that shotgun shack in Rich, he 'soon became acquainted with the semi-feral dogs who roamed free across the fields in what was more or less a pack'. He started giving them dog food, soon amounting to 50lb a week.

'They followed me around, and they were a lot of company – tall dogs, short ones, relatively friendly dogs and big, rough dogs you could not touch. They walked with me in the fields at night and when I couldn't see them, I could hear them all around me, breathing and snuffling along in the dark.'

These dogs have an immediate walk-on in the novel he was then writing. When Crawford visits Will Graham on Sugarloaf Key in Florida, he too has befriended some strays. 'Three remarkably ugly dogs wandered up and flopped to the ground around the table. "My God," Crawford said. "These are probably dogs," Graham explained. "People dump small ones here all the time. I can give away the cute ones. The rest stay around and get to be the big ones."' At the very end of *The Silence of the Lambs*, Clarice sleeps in 'the silence of the lambs' but with 'several large dogs'.

Harris uses animals to give his picture of the conditions of human life. Or, his picture of human life has been moulded not only by human behaviour but also by animal life. The food chain is his starting-point. In *Red Dragon*, the habit is muted. Few animals appear in the actual level of the narrative, by Harris's standards, although plenty compared with most novels. There are those dogs. As Graham leaves after his first talk with Crawford, it is said: 'Far out past the tidal flats, bait fish leaped for their lives.' When he comes back, there's a brief paragraph where his arms remind Molly of those of an ape, she goes out to feed those dogs, and 'moths batted softly against the screens'. The texture of this is unique to Harris. Moths always signify metamorphosis in his work, and metamorphosis is the fantasy that drives the monsters.

Later, there's the episode of Reba's blind caress of the anaesthetised tiger, the public version of Dolarhyde's identity as a big predator. 'She gripped the pelt and fur sprang between her fingers. In the very presence of the tiger her face grew pink and she lapsed into blindisms, inappropriate facial movements she had schooled herself against.'

There are other observations. Will Graham in the murder house: 'Sitting in the dark he sensed madness like a bloodhound sniffs a shirt.' He believes it was Mrs

Leeds who attracted the killer to the family. 'Graham felt that it was she who drew the monster, as surely as a singing cricket attracts death from the red-eyed fly.' Later, there's a reported comment about Graham from another police officer: 'It's like having a king snake under the house. They may not see him much, but it's nice to know he's there to eat the moccasin.' (It's a version of the comment about Kabakov, in *Black Sunday*, reported back to him by Rachel – 'he was saying that if real peace ever comes they'll have to gas you like a war dog'.) In the final scene, Graham zings out the brains of the broken-backed chicken snake and the bream rises to them in the pond. It's not in *Hannibal* that brains are first eaten.

Red Dragon and *The Silence of the Lambs* have plots that are not dissimilar. A serial killer is at work, nurturing his malign fantasy of transformation, from one murder to the next. We learn his identity before those trying to catch him do. Agents from the FBI try to find him and in the course of their quest go to interview Dr Lecter who toys with them. In both cases, the agents finally confront the monster themselves and are nearly killed by him.

Red Dragon is already a masterpiece of its kind; *The Silence of the Lambs* is yet better. One reason is that in *Red Dragon* Harris did not seem to know quite what to do with the most powerful character he had created (or, as he would see it, who had come to him), Dr Lecter. In *The Silence of the Lambs* he found out.

Six: Dr Lecter

In *Red Dragon*, Hannibal Lecter fades out of the action halfway, after having tipped off Dolarhyde about Will Graham's home address. Will Graham only goes in to see him the once.

He appears in one more brief scene with Chilton and features subsequently only through two letters to Will Graham. His prose is distinctive: concise, rhythmic, insistent, repeating words as he drives home his unwelcome insights. It is Dr Lecter's style always to reiterate the name of the person he is addressing as he speaks or writes to them (moving in the course of his second meeting with Starling from 'Officer Starling' to 'Clarice').

In his first letter to Will Graham, he tells him: 'You know, Will, you worry too much. You'd be so much more comfortable if you relaxed with yourself.

'We don't invent our natures, Will; they're issued to us along with our lungs and pancreas and everything else. Why fight it? I want to help you, Will...'

Dr Lecter of course, would know about these internal organs. Lecter sends another letter to Will Graham, as he recovers in hospital after Dolarhyde's final attack, again insisting on their resemblance. 'Dear Will, Here we are, you and I, languishing in our hospitals. You have your pain and I am without my books.' Crawford destroys the letter, before Graham can read it. He, in turn, will receive Lecter's next letter, early in *The Silence of the Lambs*, apparently commiserating with the terminal illness of his wife, Bella.

> O wrangling schools, that search what fire
> Shall burn this world, had none the wit
> Unto this knowledge to aspire
> That this her fever might be it?

> I'm so sorry about Bella, Jack.
> Hannibal Lecter.

With horrible aptness, Lecter quotes, from memory, 'A Fever' by John Donne. He has grasped that Donne's conceit, that the lover's death would amount to the end of his world, may be the truth for Crawford. (Donne supplies also one of the epigraphs of *The Silence of the Lambs*: 'Need I look upon a death's head in a ring, that have one in my face?' – half a sentence from the *Devotions, Expostulation 16*, which continues with equal aptness, 'or go for death to my neighbour's house that have him in my bosom?')

Lecter's range of reference is impressive. He is, precisely, a great and rapacious reader, of people and pages both – which is perhaps why he can discard the former as easily as the latter. ('The Devil criticises the universe like a bad book,' said Madame de Staël.)

Much print has been expended on attempting to identify 'the real Hannibal Lecter', the genuine serial killer on whom he may have been based. Harris himself appears to have mentioned the Mexican doctor he interviewed in prison to one of his English publishers, Helen Fraser. To a librarian in Cleveland, Mississippi, Harris mentioned a local killer, William Coyner, as his inspiration. In 1934, Coyner escaped from an Indiana prison and went on a murder and cannibalism spree in Cleveland. When he was captured, 200 armed police guarded him; he went to the gallows. It seems likely he would still have functioned as a bogeyman in the area ten or 15 years later when Harris was a boy.

When these searches for the 'original Hannibal Lecter' have not prospered, reporters have been sent round the world to interview frankly unrelated murderers and, where possible, cannibals, as generic 'real Hannibal Lecters', including, most recently, 29-year-old

Jason Ricketts from Caerphilly in South Wales who murdered and eviscerated a cellmate in Cardiff Prison, mistaking his spleen for his heart. Anonymous early Britons have also been nominated. A cannibalised thigh bone was discovered in Gloucestershire, carbon-dated to the first century, prompting a forensic archaeologist at Bournemouth University, Professor Margaret Cox, to say 'this is obviously an isolated case of aberrant behaviour, what you might call a British Hannibal Lecter'.

It's all misguided. Hannibal Lecter not only lives in books, he came out of books too.

Admittedly, it does seem that the story given so surprisingly and perhaps unwisely in *Hannibal*, of the murder and eating of Lecter's younger sister Mischa 'in 1944 after the Eastern Front collapsed', may have been modelled on a story told by the Ukrainian murderer Andrei Chikatilo, whose crimes were made public in 1992. Chikatilo claimed to have been influenced in his crimes by the fact that his elder brother had been kidnapped and killed by a gang of the cannibals who roamed the Ukraine in the 1930s. However, no proof of this elder brother's existence has been found and Chikatilo was not a witness to trust.

True, too, that the secondary villains of *Red Dragon* and *The Silence of the Lambs* were modelled to some extent on famous cases. Jame Gumb, for example, incorporates elements of Ed Gein, Ted Bundy and Ed Kemper, all murderers interviewed for the Behavioral Science Unit by Douglas and Ressler.

John Douglas mentions in passing that Harris picked up on the story of Ed Gein, 'while sitting in on our classes at Quantico'. Gein began as a graverobber: 'His particular interest was the corpse's skin, which he removed, tanned, and draped across his own body, in addition to furnishing a tailor's dummy and various home furnishings. At one point, he had considered a sex-change operation – still revolutionary in the Midwest of the 1950s – and when that seemed impractical, decided on the next best thing, which was making himself a woman suit out of real women. Some speculate he was trying to become his dead, domineering mother.' His case was used for Robert Bloch's *Psycho*, filmed by Hitchcock, long before Harris commandeered it for Gumb. Gein, detained in an institution for the criminally insane since 1958, was interviewed in his seventies for the BSU programme. Ressler says he showed Harris specific cases 'including that of Ed Gein' too.

Ted Bundy's method of operation included appearing defenceless to his victims by wearing an arm-cast – which he would then use to club them – as Jame

81

Gumb does when abducting Catherine Martin. Ressler interviewed him for his BSU project without getting anywhere. Indeed Bundy alarmed Ressler by appearing familiar with his books, too. 'He... convinced someone else in the Bureau to obtain from me an autographed copy of my textbook on serial murder, and had it in his cell at the time he went to the electric chair. He even quoted from it in his last videotaped interview.' Ed Kemper, another interviewee, had murdered his grandparents as an adolescent but had then been let out of the asylum as a young man and killed many times again, a history given to Gumb too.

But Hannibal Lecter plays a different role in Harris's novels from the other killers and he is not based on criminological research. In truth, the Hannibal Lecter stories have about the same connection to social reality as, say, the stories of Bluebeard or Dracula. Like those stories, they still have, of course, an acute psychological reality.

There's a brisk account of this disjunction between fact and imagination in the first chapter of *Hunting Humans*, a recent study of real-life serial killers by Elliott Leyton. Of *Hannibal*, he says: 'If it is an artful thriller, it is a terrible piece of criminology. Indeed, the theatrical qualities that make these books and films such exciting tales are, unfortunately, the same qualities that make them disastrously bad criminology... The primary nonsense dispensed by this genre is the supposition that serial murderers are Supermen, even Super Heroes.' As Leyton explains, real serial murderers are 'usually without intellectual or physical attainments, they are often uneducated and virtually illiterate... In sum, they are dull, unimaginative, socially defective, vengeful, self-absorbed and self-pitying human beings. In fact, there is no connection whatever between what serial murderers are really like and the way they are portrayed in films and books.' Dennis Nilsen's confidant, Brian Masters, has said much the same several times in denunciation of the Hannibal Lecter stories.

These experts have, then, nearly arrived at the wisdom of the French philosopher Simone Weil. In *Morality and Literature,* published pseudonymously in 1944, she wrote: 'Nothing is so beautiful and wonderful, nothing is so continually fresh and surprising, so full of sweet and perpetual ecstasy, as the good. No desert is so dreary, monotonous and boring as evil. This is the truth about authentic good and evil. With fictional good and evil it is the other way round. Fictional good is boring and flat, while fictional evil is varied and intriguing, attractive, profound, and full of charm.' Weil's conclusion, by the way, was that 'immorality is inseparable from literature', except in writers of genius. 'Although the works of these men are made out of words there is present in them the force of gravity which governs our souls... There, good and evil appear in their truth.' On which side of this divide the works of Thomas Harris are to be located, the reader is invited to decide for herself. Or to read on.

Lecter's true antecedents are not then in the annals of crime. They are to be found elsewhere altogether, in fable and fiction. He is a compound of evil. He is Satan and he is the Serpent. He is the Vampire. He is the Beast to Clarice's Beauty. In *Hannibal*, all these identifications are teasingly introduced – as well as a psychological explanation of his make-up, in the form of that unfortunate childhood.

One of Lecter's most obvious fictional precursors is Sherlock Holmes, and before him, therefore, Poe's Dupin. Many of Lecter's observations are pure Holmes in style, if not content: After telling Graham, by way of a greeting, that he's wearing the 'same atrocious aftershave' he wore in court, in very Holmesian fashion, he notices that he is 'very tan' and that his hands are rough, as if to work out where he is now living.

Informed by Clarice Starling that Multiple Miggs said he could smell her cunt, Lecter replies: 'I see. I myself cannot. You use Evyan skin cream, and sometimes you wear L'Air du Temps, but not today.' On their next meeting, he detects a Band-Aid under her clothes.

Compare Holmes on his first meeting with Watson in *A Study in Scarlet*: ' "You have been in Afghanistan, I perceive." "How on earth did you know that?" I asked in astonishment.' When, at their next meeting, Holmes explains his deductions, the amazed Watson says, rightly enough, 'You remind me of Edgar Allan Poe's Dupin. I had no idea that such individuals did exist outside of stories.'

Conan Doyle admitted that Poe had been his great influence: 'Poe is the master of all. To him must be ascribed the monstrous progeny of writers on the detection of crime... Each may find some little development of his own, but his main art must trace back to those admirable stories of Monsieur Dupin, so wonderful in their masterful force, their reticence, their quick dramatic point. After all, mental acuteness is the one quality which can be ascribed to the ideal detective, and when that has once been admirably done, succeeding writers must necessarily be content for all time to follow in the same main track.' Unless, that is, the mental acuteness is ascribed not to a detective, but to a criminal, tangentially engaged in the detection of other criminals. Here's one straight line of descent for Hannibal Lecter: Professor Moriarty and Sherlock Holmes combining their talents.

Another bloodline passes through Bram Stoker's *Dracula*. We learn in *Hannibal* that, like Dracula, Lecter is a Central European aristocrat. His father, too, was a Count and he believes himself to be descended from a 12th-century Tuscan named Bevisangue (blood-drinker). Like Dracula, Lecter drains his victims. After meeting him for the first time, Clarice Starling feels 'suddenly empty, as though she had given blood'.

Lecter, like Dracula, has superhuman strength; he commands the beasts; and he lives in the night. Barney, the warder, tells Clarice on her second visit that Lecter is always awake at night, 'even when his lights are off'. Many of his physical attributes resemble those of Dracula. 'His cultured voice has a slight metallic rasp beneath it, possibly from disuse', we are told in *The Silence of the Lambs*. Dracula, says Stoker, speaks in a 'harsh, metallic whisper'. Dracula's eyes are red, Jonathan Harker realises when he first meets him, in the guise of a coachman. Later, when he sees Dracula with his female acolytes, he says: 'The red light in them was lurid, as if the flames of hell-fire blazed behind them.' So too: 'Dr Lecter's eyes are maroon and they reflect the light in pinpoints of red. Sometimes the points of light seem to fly like sparks to his centre.'

Dracula has, of course, 'peculiarly sharp white teeth'. Dr Lecter's teeth are noted but they're pointedly not fangs, just 'small white teeth', although he too uses them to terrible effect – and, of course, consumes his victims. Dracula has a combination of 'extraordinary pallor' and lips of 'remarkable ruddiness'. Lecter, too, combines pallor and red lips: 'The only colours in his cell were his hair and eyes and his red mouth, in a face so long out of the sun it leached into the surrounding whiteness...' There seems little doubt that Harris's success in adding so dramatically to our stock of monsters drew on Bram Stoker's earlier triumph in refining and perfecting the myth of the vampire (first brought to a large public in 1820 by Byron's sidekick Dr John Polidori).

In *Hannibal*, Harris tips the wink a little to Dracula. Much of the business of Dracula is taken up transporting the Count's boxes of soil from Transylvania to his properties in Essex and Piccadilly. Dr Lecter's homemaking is more elaborate. Chapter 54 of *Hannibal* – the chapter which proclaims 'Dr Lecter very much liked to shop' – begins: 'It is an axiom of behavioural science that vampires are territorial, while cannibals range widely across the country. The nomadic existence held little appeal for Dr Lecter.' Setting aside the question of what behavioural science can say about imaginary monsters, it's a nice nod to Lecter's precursor. (It may, however, just be a coincidence that among the insects

Dracula sends in to his deranged acolyte Renfield in the asylum is '*Acherontia atropos* of the Sphinges – what we call the 'Death's-head Hawk Moth', the European version of the insect that alerts Clarice Starling to the identity of Jame Gumb.)

Lecter has taken on a fuller and more florid existence in each successive book. In *Red Dragon*, still only five-fingered, he seems a relatively plain fellow, compared to the lifestyle fiend who emerges in *Hannibal*, bedecked too with a dizzying plurality of historical, genealogical and mythological attributes.

Throughout *Hannibal*, he is, for example, Satan, the only other figure of evil who is wise as well as malevolent, who understands but does not sympathise. A gypsy says so plainly. 'That is the Devil... Shaitan, Son of the Morning, I've seen him now.' And there are many other teasing references, as when Lecter retrieves a new identity from 'the Devil's Armour with its horned helmet' and its 'gauntlet cuffs... stuck where shoes should be, at the ends of the greaves, suggesting the cloven hooves of Satan'.

Then again in *Hannibal,* Lecter is the Beast and Clarice is Beauty – only this time it is the Beast who changes Beauty, not Beauty the Beast. The story is explicitly raised when Mason Verger asks Dr Doemling, the duff psychologist, what Lecter wants to do to

Clarice: 'Does he want to fuck her or kill her, or eat her, or what?' Doemling says probably all three, in whatever order. 'No matter how the tabloids – and tabloid mentalities – might want to romanticise it, and try to make it Beauty and the Beast, his object is her degradation, her suffering and her death.'

In fact, Clarice's time in Lecter's care in his house on the Maryland shore is unmistakably modelled on 'La Belle et la Bête' by Jeanne-Marie Leprince de Beaumont (1756, see *The Great Fairy Tale Tradition*, edited by Jack Zipes, Norton, 2001). Beauty, like Clarice, is devoted to her father and that is why she goes to the Beast's palace. The Beast cooks marvellously for her and she says to herself: 'It's clear that the Beast is providing such a lovely feast to fatten me up before eating me.'

The Beast prepares a magnificent room for her – what struck her most of all was a large library, a harpsichord and numerous books on music. 'She hears an excellent concert', just as Lecter plays the harpsichord to Clarice.

But Beauty pines to see her father and the Beast arranges for her to do so in a mirror – just as Lecter arranges a spectral visitation from Clarice's dead father. ' "Beauty," the monster said to her, "would you mind if I watch you dine?" ' Just so, as Clarice eats Krendler's brains, 'Dr Lecter found the shine of butter sauce on her lip intensely moving.' Then, of course, the Beast asks Beauty to be his wife and she 'nearly died of fright'. She'll come round to the idea, as Starling does.

When he allows her to make a visit to her father, the Beast supplies Beauty with 'dresses trimmed with gold and diamonds'. Just so, Lecter dresses Clarice in 'a long dinner gown' and gives her 'earrings with pendant cabochon emeralds'. 'Clarice Starling smiled at him then, the cabochons caught the firelight and the monster was lost in self-congratulation at his own exquisite taste and cunning.' Beauty releases the Beast from the spell he is under. Hannibal Lecter, however, puts Clarice under his spell. Reading these two stories together, there is no mistaking the path being followed. We are in Harris's footsteps here.

Another of Lecter's literary sources is a little trickier. The name and notion of Hannibal Lecter grew – at some level of consciousness, at some stage of development, perhaps the earliest – from Baudelaire's great poem of preface to *Les Fleurs du Mal*, 'Au Lecteur' (To The Reader).

There seems little doubt of this, although Harris, while trailing his coat about other writers, has been careful to avoid referring to those, such as Poe, Conan Doyle and Baudelaire, from whom he has taken most.

Such a genealogy may sound fanciful for a thriller but Harris is in fact a deeply literary writer. In 'An Ideal English Class Syllabus for 9th Graders', he says firmly: 'Every day a poem in a foreign language.'

Baudelaire published 'Au Lecteur' in 1855 in the *Revue des Deux Mondes* and then placed it at the head of the first edition of *Les Fleurs du Mal* in June 1857. In this assault of a poem, Baudelaire declares himself to be writing only for those readers who resemble him. It begins in midstream, with a fiercely inclusive 'we' ;

> *La sottise, l'erreur, le péché, la lésine,*
> *Occupent nos esprits et travaillent nos corps,*
> *Et nous alimentons nos aimables remords,*
> *Comme les mendiants nourissent leur vermine.*
>
> [Stupidity, error, sin, and meanness possess our minds and work on our bodies, and we feed our fond remorse as beggars suckle their own lice.]

At once, the reader is recruited to horror. Instead of being carefully approached and seductively addressed, as would be normal in a poem of dedication, he has been made, before he knows it, to utter, alongside the poet, the most savage confession of sin. So the poem continues, making us declare ourselves captives of 'Satan Trismégiste':

C'est le Diable qui tient les fils qui nous remuent!
Aux objets répugnants nous trouvons des appas;
Chaque jour vers l'Enfer nous descendons d'un pas,
Sans horreur, à travers des ténèbres qui puent.

[It's the Devil who pulls the strings that make us dance:
we take delight in loathsome things; each day we take a
further step to Hell, yet feel no horror as we descend
through stinking gloom.]

Baudelaire leads us past one loathsome thing to another. Eventually, we arrive at the vice that is worse than
all the rest.

Mais parmi les chacals, les panthères, les lices,
Les singes, les scorpions, les vautours, les serpents,
Les monstres glapissants, hurlants, grognants, rampants,
Dans la ménagerie infâme de nos vices,

Il en est un plus laid, plus méchant, plus immonde!
Quoiqu'il ne pousse ni grands gestes ni grands cris,
Il ferait volontiers de la terre un débris
Et dans un bâillement avalerait le monde;

C'est l'Ennui!...

[But among the jackals, panthers, bitch-hounds, monkeys,
scorpions, vultures, snakes, and monsters that scream
and howl and grunt and crawl in the sordid menagerie of

our vices, there is one even uglier and more wicked and filthier than all the rest! He would happily reduce the earth to rubble and swallow the world in a yawn. 'C'est l'Ennui!']

It is boredom, *taedium vitae*, that drives all our sins.

Suddenly, in his last two lines, Baudelaire drops the compelling 'we' that has dominated the poem and turns on the reader with an intimate, uninvited second person singular, before offering to embrace him again:

Tu le connais, lecteur, ce monstre délicat,
– Hypocrite lecteur, – mon semblable, – mon frère!

[You know him, reader, that fastidious monster
– you hypocritical reader – my similar – my brother!]

Harris surely had these great lines in his mind when Lecter was first coalescing in his mind. They underlie the nature of the character as potently as Blake's painting of the Great Red Dragon structures the madness of Francis Dolarhyde. It's possible to see the whole phenomenon of Hannibal Lecter as a fantastic gloss on this poem and *Les Fleurs du Mal*.

The chime of '*hypocrite lecteur*' with Hannibal Lecter is obvious enough. Then again Lecter is precisely a fastidious monster; one who would gladly reduce the earth to ruin. On Lecter's first appearance, he insists to

Will Graham 'WE'RE JUST ALIKE', almost a translation of the poem's climax. But there are more significant ways in which Harris develops this theme.

Lecter's a lecteur. It's been noted that Lecter is always a reader, a quoter and a writer. He lives in literature. Like the infant Thomas Harris, as described by his mother, he always has his nose in a book.

Lecter tests Clarice as a reader when, on their second meeting, he gives her the religious maniac Sammie's poem on a piece of paper and she is made to perform a little practical criticism on it, noting the 'verse changes' and the 'management of rhyme'. When she sees him next, he's reading his correspondence and holds up a finger for silence until he has finished.

Even in the cell in the Memphis jailhouse, Lecter manages to have 'a number of books' and finishes his page and marks his place, before speaking to Starling. 'Dumas tells us that the addition of a crow to bouillon in the fall, when the crow has fattened on juniper berries, greatly improves the colour and flavour of stock. How do you like it in the soup, Clarice?' (Dumas does indeed say *'le corbeau, en novembre et décembre, ajoutent beaucoup à la sapidité et l'arôme du bouillon'* in *Le Grand Dictionnaire de Cuisine*, the book Lecter is reading when first seen in *Red Dragon*.) Lecter is telling her about this because in his mind, Starling is akin to a corvid herself. In an earlier chapter, she has remembered a crow mottled black and white that stole from the motel cleaning carts where her mother was working when she told Clarice she was being sent away to Montana. She dreams of it still. Such arcane but phenomenally connected details animate all Harris's writing.

Then Lecter tells Starling: '"I've read the cases, Clarice, have you? Everything you need to know to find him is right there."' All he really wants is for her to be a better reader. He ridicules Crawford for a speech to the National Police Academy and says he 'copies his philosophy out of *Bartlett's Familiar*, I think. If he understood Marcus Aurelius, he might solve his case.' Clarice asks how and Lecter responds tartly: '"When you show the odd flash of contextual intelligence, I forget your generation can't read, Clarice."' (Again, the passage he refers to in Marcus Aurelius does exist, just as he says.)

Lecter also instructs the warder, Barney, on his reading, we may realise, when Clarice notices that 'A paperback book was wrapped around Barney's massive index finger as he held his place. It was Jane Austen's *Sense and Sensibility*.' Later, in *Hannibal*, we learn that Lecter helped Barney with his correspondence courses and showed him Socrates and much else: 'He showed me a whole world, literally, of stuff – Suetonius, Gibbon, all that.'

Given Lecter's preparedness to share his reading thus, it is worth remarking that almost the only piece of journalism or writing outside his books that Harris has done since finding fame, was a reading list – that piece for a teen magazine: 'An Ideal English Class Syllabus for 9th Graders'.

Harris ends this piece by suggesting we should take a look at the plaque that Nasa puts on the side of the deep-space probes to tell other beings what we are: 'bilaterally symmetrical, sexually differentiated bipeds located on one of the outer spirals of the Milky Way, capable of recognising the prime numbers and moved by one extraordinary quality that lasts longer than all our other urges – curiosity.

'Curiosity. All we can ever do is tickle one another's curiosity, because there isn't time to say much, and a lot of what we know to say may not be true.'

Curiosity, then, is the opposite of Ennui. It is the corrective that Harris when speaking in his own voice recommends to the boredom that breeds monsters. Remember that Lecter tilts his head when he asks a question, 'as though he were screwing an augur of curiosity into your face'.

Barney warns Dr Chilton, as he says goodbye to

Lecter, that his new guards don't know how to deal with him. 'You think they'll treat him right? You know how he is – you have to threaten him with boredom. That's all he's afraid of. Slapping him around's no good.' But ennui is not just his fear – 'Any rational society would either kill me or give me my books' – it's his origin. Lecter himself uses his own boredom as a threat to others. When he is extracting the story of *The Silence of the Lambs* from Clarice and she is not delivering what he wants, he says: 'If you're tired, we could talk toward the end of the week. I'm rather bored myself.'

Lecter is the face that looks back at us out of our own boredom. He is our monster, the evil we embrace for our diversion. And he feeds on us.

In *Hannibal*, this idea is made explicit in a manner distinctively reminiscent of the accusation embedded in 'Au Lecteur'. Lecter attends the exhibition of Atrocious Torture Instruments but not to look at the exhibits. He faces the other way, back at the spectators, for his thrills. 'The essence of the worst, the true asafoetida of the human spirit, is not found in the Iron Maiden or the whetted edge; Elemental Ugliness is found in the faces of the crowd', the oracular narrative voice proclaims.

For his part, Lecter 'is registering aspects of

damnation from the avid faces of the voyeurs as they press around the torture instruments and press against each other in steamy, goggle-eyed frottage, hair rising on their forearms, breath hot on one another's neck and cheeks'. Just so when Harris went to the FBI, he was learning at least as much about the agents as about the criminals they were discussing. After *The Silence of the Lambs*, there was much head-nodding when it was learned that Harris was attending the 'Mostro' trial in Italy. When *Hannibal* appeared, it became clear that once again he had been looking more at the police for the creation of Pazzi than at the accused.

Harris has made one direct statement on the record about his relationship to Lecter, in a video made for the sales staff of his publisher, aptly filmed in the extraordinary butterfly house at Syon Park near Heathrow in London. He called Lecter a friend and spoke of him as an independent presence. 'He's immensely amusing company. I work in this little office and I'm always glad when he shows up. He can be difficult company and I'm glad when he leaves too. People always ask me most about him, I can't say where he came from. What he is, in the most general terms, is a worthy adversary. He is the adversary for anything like kindness and hope. He is not specifically modelled after anybody but I think if you look around the world you can see plenty of

sources where the darkness of Dr Lecter came from...
he's the dark side of the world. He's probably the
wickedest man I've ever heard of – at the same time he
tells the truth and he says some things that I suppose
we would all like to say. It's his contention that the
asylum is the only place in the world where free speech
is practised. He may be right...'

Harris also nicely pretended that Lecter was outside
his control. 'People ask me if he's coming back but I
don't know. He doesn't return my phone calls. He's a
man who has to amuse himself...'

But perhaps Thomas Harris 'can't say' where Lecter
came from only in the sense that he can't permit himself
to say. Then again look: in the Acknowledgements to
Hannibal, he has now said it: 'The wickedness herein I
took from my own stock.'

Seven: The Silence of the Lambs

The Silence of the Lambs was published in 1988 (in the
States), seven years after *Red Dragon.* It is impossible
to read it and not recognise it as a masterpiece of its
form. It is relentlessly suspenseful and, strange to say,
this effect does not disappear or even much diminish
on rereading, when the outcome is known. Indeed

rereading *The Silence of the Lambs* always reveals new intricacies of pattern, carefully placed echoes, symmetries and clues. It's not easily exhausted, this book.

Yet on first encounter the story is so compelling that it's almost impossible to take it slowly. Indeed some of Harris's writing is so tense that the eye won't stay on the lines but leaps ahead. *The Silence of the Lambs* functions equally well as a pure thriller and as a sophisticated literary text. Harris has pulled off a considerable structural feat here, embedding his subtleties and arabesques, his allusions and references so deep into the text that they do not snag the superficial reader yet reward the most attentive one. Harris has developed his craft a significant stage further than in *Red Dragon*. He seems here in complete command of his material and his manner in a way few novelists attain.

Harris has offered us a few clues to the book's origin. In the omnibus preface, he again feigns passivity in the face of his characters. 'When I started *The Silence of the Lambs*, I did not know that Dr Lecter would return. I had always liked the character of Dahlia Iyad in *Black Sunday* and wanted to do a novel with a strong woman as the central character. So I began with Clarice Starling and, not two pages into the novel, I found she had to go visit the doctor. I admired Clarice Starling enormously and I think I suffered some feelings of jealousy at the ease with which Dr Lecter saw into her, when it was so difficult for me.'

It's worth noting that there are many strong women characters in Harris's novels: Dahlia Iyad in *Black Sunday*, Molly Foster Graham and Reba McClane in *Red Dragon*, Clarice Starling, Ardelia Mapp, Senator Martin and Catherine Martin in *The Silence of the Lambs*. In a piece for *Salon* magazine, Joyce Millman chose Clarice Starling as her favourite literary heroine. 'Has a heroine ever been as beloved by her creator as Clarice? Thomas Harris treats Clarice with exquisite tenderness and respect... In order to rise above her humble beginnings and become the woman she wants to be, Clarice must confront the thing she fears the most, which is her own helplessness. With the utmost gentleness, Harris leads her to her nightmare, and that nightmare is what gives *The Silence of the Lambs* its heft and snap: Hannibal Lecter.' The piece was written before the appearance of *Hannibal*, naturally.

Taking a very young woman as the lead made *The Silence of the Lambs* even more emotionally wrenching a read than *Red Dragon*. She is Harris's sole young protagonist, still unformed. Whereas Will Graham is already deep into damage, Starling is just starting out, still in the process of discovering what she can make of herself both personally and professionally. She is not yet a qualified agent but she is called upon to do what the Bureau with all its resources cannot. It's just a great adventure story in that way.

Clarice is also struggling to emerge from her background. Orphaned, she remains in thrall to the image of her father, the murdered marshal. As she shuttles between Jack Crawford and Hannibal Lecter, they both act as mentors, substitute fathers, to her. Then again, her age and sex also give her an immediate identification with Jame Gumb's victims, both those already dead and Catherine Martin, waiting in the pit. In trying to save Catherine, she is also trying to slay her own monsters. She has not yet had to realise, as Kabakov and Will Graham know to their cost, that the skills and inclinations that make her a good hunter are qualities she has in common with the predators she is hunting.

Clarice is changing and growing throughout the book. The second serial killer of *The Silence of the Lambs*, Jame Gumb, however, is another of Harris's monsters driven by a delusion of change, of becoming another kind of being. (Lecter just is what he is – he has no such dream of becoming different.) Gumb's dream is incarnated for him by the moths with their genuine power to metamorphose – and he attempts to emulate them by the appallingly literal method of putting himself in the skins of others. Like Dolarhyde before him, he has had his frightful moment of revelation.

It was this aspect of *The Silence of the Lambs* that Harris chose to emphasise in explaining the book, in a true storyteller's fashion, for the salesmen in the Syon Park video:

A chrysalis of a death's-head moth plays a large part in the story. The chrysalis is change and Jame Gumb wanted very much to change. At his lowest point, Gumb – fired from his job, tossed aside by his lover – opens a suitcase he had stolen from his employer hoping there would be some jewellery in it. It was full of dead butterflies. He sat there despondent in this terrible room in San Francisco, looking at this suitcase and there was movement in it. He heard a scratching noise and a moth climbed out. It was a chrysalis that had been thrown into the suitcase and this moth had hatched in transit, gnawed his way out. He came out, spread his wings and they dried and Gumb, in that moment in his room, had a terrible epiphany. He saw that he could change. He was determined to change. He did not care what it cost anybody.

Lecter explains to Clarice why she has found a chrysalis in the throat of Gumb's victims. 'The significance of the chrysalis is change. Worm into butterfly, or moth. Billy thinks he wants to change. Hence the large victims – he has to have things that fit. The number of victims suggests he may see it as a series of moults.' (In one of the arcane verbal echoes that Harris delights in, that word has already been applied to Jack Crawford. At the start of the book, Starling notices that something is wrong with him, that his clever dress-sense has left him: 'Now he was neat but drab, as though he were moulting.' Similarly, the name of the Smithsonian scientist with whom Clarice spends the weekend at the end of the book contains another minor shock. Noble Pilcher is called Pilch for short by his colleague: a 'pilch' is precisely 'an outer garment made of skin dressed with the hair'. He may not be ideal boyfriend material.)

The insane Gumb has no potential for change. Raspail, talking to Lecter just before Lecter killed him, said: 'Jame is not really gay, you know, it's just something he picked up in jail. He's not anything, really, just a sort of total lack that he wants to fill, and so angry. You always felt the room was a little emptier when he came in.'

Clarice Starling, however, is genuinely metamorphosing, as Lecter immediately sees and admires in her. In their first meeting he recognises her attraction, her courage and ambition, but what he fastens on to most sharply is her taste, not yet formed but already developing. He compliments her, in his best malign-Sherlock fashion, on her bag.

'You brought your best bag, didn't you?'

'Yes.' It was true. She had saved for the classic casual handbag, and it was the best item she owned.

'It's much better than your shoes.'

'Maybe they'll catch up.'

'I have no doubt of it.'

A little further into the conversation he pulls off another Sherlock trick, telling her she has a string of gold add-a-beads back in her room which now seem tacky to her.

'All those tedious thank-yous, permitting all that sincere fumbling, getting all sticky once for every bead. Tedious. Tedious. Bo-o-o-o-r-i-ing. Being smart spoils a lot of things, doesn't it? And taste isn't kind. When you think about this conversation, you'll remember the dumb animal hurt in his face when you got rid of him.

'If the add-a-beads got tacky, what else will as you go along? You wonder don't you, at night?' Dr Lecter asked in the kindest of tones.

Dr Lecter's verbal assaults are as decisive and radical as his physical ones. It is taste that will eventually bring Clarice Starling to him. Taste is everything to Dr Lecter in every sense. And taste isn't kind.

Lecter entices Clarice by offering her what she loves

the most, advancement. In exchange, she must give of herself, though through the bars it can only be in words. The transaction is somewhere between a parody of psychoanalysis and the bargain struck between Faust and Mephistopheles. He sucks out her inner life, as he trades the information she needs for her disclosures to him, 'strictly COD'. 'What's your worst memory of childhood?' he asks. 'Quicker than that... I'm not interested in your worst invention.' She describes her father's death. He is satisfied. 'You've been very frank, Clarice. I always know. I think it would be quite something to know you in private life.' He will.

On their fourth meeting, in the Memphis jailhouse, she tells him the story of the horse, Hannah, about to be taken for slaughter, and of the lambs screaming as they were slaughtered. She could rescue only the horse.

> 'You still wake up sometimes, don't you? Wake up in the iron dark with the lambs screaming?'
>
> 'Sometimes.'
>
> 'Do you think if you caught Buffalo Bill yourself and if you made Catherine all right, you could make the lambs stop screaming, do you think they'd be all right too and you wouldn't wake up again in the dark and hear the lambs screaming? Clarice?'
>
> 'Yes. I don't know. Maybe.'

'Thank you, Clarice.' Dr Lecter seemed oddly at peace.

He has plucked out her heart. With the insight he has given her, Starling finds Jame Gumb and rescues Catherine Martin, while Lecter escapes.

Lecter makes one more contact with her in this book, through another of his letters. 'The lambs will stop for now. But, Clarice, you judge yourself with all the mercy of the dungeon scales at Threave; you'll have to earn it again and again, the blessed silence. Because it's the plight that drives you, seeing the plight, and the plight will not end, ever.'

In another of Harris's intricacies, 'plight' folds back to the previous use of the word to describe Bach's *Goldberg Variations* which Lecter listens to in his cage as he prepares to escape. 'The music, beautiful beyond plight and time, filled the bright cage and the room where the warders sat.' The book is full of such little shocks and premonitions that can only be picked up on rereading. For instance, Lecter has up on the wall in his cell his own picture of Florence, 'seen from the Belvedere'. It is in Belvedere, Ohio, that Starling will find Gumb. Again, in his pep-talk to Starling about managing her anger, Crawford tells her to see past it to the prize: 'Catherine Martin's life. And Buffalo Bill's hide on the barn door.' She is to find Jame Gumb (aka Buffalo Bill) has been sewing leather under the name of 'Mr Hide'. And so on.

To unfold all the intricacies and allusions in *The Silence of the Lambs* would take more space than the novel itself occupies. There are some useful websites publishing ongoing annotations to *The Silence of the Lambs* (and, now, *Hannibal* too) and they keep coming up with surprising observations and connections. None of these connections drives the plot, which functions perfectly without them. They are there as part of Harris's own passion for making perfect. It is a passion his murderers share less successfully. Mr Gumb: 'His ideal was a seamless garment. This was not possible. He was determined, though, that the bodice front be absolutely seamless and without blemish.'

We learn of Dr Lecter near the end of *Hannibal*: 'Ever, he sought pattern.' This is Harris's commitment as a novelist too. That's why Bach is esteemed by Lecter, and, we can be sure, by Harris, as 'beyond plight and time'. Beyond plight and time we cannot be, but a work of art can. In *Hannibal,* we hear Bach again, played this time not by Glenn Gould but by Lecter himself. 'Bach's *Goldberg Variations* played, not perfectly, but exceedingly well, with an engaging understanding of the music. Played not perfectly, but exceedingly well; there is perhaps a slight stiffness in the left hand.' The sentence structure emulates the movement of the music, a trick Harris loves.

It is this ability to use his prose to capture the movement of a mind, including a mad mind, that makes his murderers so completely unnerving. He leaves no distance at all between the reader and the insanity, even though the prose remains third-person. The chapters in *The Silence of the Lambs* that take us inside the head of Jame Gumb are among Harris's most horrifying because they make us, as we read, think as he does. 'Watching Catherine, playing the infrared flashlight up and down her, Mr Gumb prepares himself for the very real problems ahead.

'The human skin is fiendishly difficult to deal with if your standards are as high as Mr Gumb's. There are fundamental structural decisions to make, and the first one is where to put the zipper.'

Mr Gumb himself always refers to Catherine Martin as 'it', 'the material', 'the hide'. 'He could never hear it from the kitchen even at the top of its voice, thank goodness, but he could hear it on the stairs as he went down to the basement. He had hoped it would be quiet and asleep.'

As he prepares to 'harvest the hide', he becomes overjoyed and the sentences follow his every move.

It was hard to behave in a responsible manner – he wanted to fly about the room like Danny Kaye. He laughed and blew a moth away from his face with a gentle puff of air.

'Time to start the aquarium pumps in his fresh tanks of solution. Oh, was there a nice chrysalis buried in the humus in the cage? Yes, there was.

'The pistol, now.'

Even on rereading, it remains shocking that Harris has been able to convey murderous insanity so convincingly. For he is not describing it, he is expressing it. The words embody the brutality. In such scenes, Harris has been inside these heads, a feat attributed several times to Lecter by those who meet him. *Red Dragon*: 'Graham felt that Lecter was looking through to the back of his skull. His attention felt like a fly walking around in there.'

Harris writes curiously about this phenomenon in his preface. As he worked in his cabin in the middle of the Mississippi night, he could walk out and comfortably look in on, say, Chilton.

'I found that I could leave Chilton in the cabin with the lights on and look back at him in the dark, surrounded by my friends the dogs. I was invisible then, out there in the dark, the way I am invisible to my characters when I'm in a room with them and they are deciding their fates with little or no help from me.'

When he approached Lecter, things changed. 'I was enjoying my usual immunity while working, my invisibility to Chilton and Graham and the staff, but I was not comfortable in the presence of Dr Lecter, not sure at all that the doctor could not see me. Like Graham, I found, and find, the scrutiny of Dr Lecter uncomfortable, intrusive, like the humming in your thoughts when they X-ray your head.'

This may be hokum but it's as close to an acknowledgement as Harris will give that Lecter is inside us, not out there, inside us as evil is. He looks back at us, like our own reflection. In retrospect, *The Silence of the Lambs* hints at *Hannibal* in many ways. Lecter's love of Florence has been seen. It has been made clear that the best place to look for him would be a library. Then there is the burgeoning intimacy between Clarice and Lecter. When she visits him in the Memphis jailhouse, she admits: 'They didn't send me. I just came.' He replies: 'People will say we're in love.'

Krendler, too, has been tee'd up for a return. When he finds Clarice in Catherine Martin's apartment and suspects her of thieving, she makes her mind up. 'She would never forgive Krendler for the doubt in his face. Never.' She does not. When she is thinking of her future career in the FBI, she wonders: 'Would she have to watch out for that fucking Krendler for the rest of her life?' Not quite, as it turns out.

But, most powerfully, *The Silence of the Lambs* anticipates ~~Hannibal by bringing the picture of the~~ world as a struggle for life, an arena of contest between predatory beasts, into sharper focus than before. The novel is alive with animals. There are, of course, the pastoral beasts, the horses and the lambs in Clarice's story as she tells it to Lecter. There are, too, Jame Gumb's moths both alive and dead, symbols of a transformation he will never attain.

There is, rather more opaquely, a fair amount of bird symbolism attached to Starling. She tells her story of the black and white crow. But also there are the references to doves and pigeons. When she has been sent back to school by Krendler, there is this poignant little passage:

> Then she was alone on the parking lot, with the unsteady feeling that she understood nothing at all in this world.
>
> She watched a pigeon walk around beneath the motor homes and boats. It picked up a peanut hull and put it down. The damp wind ruffled its feathers.

When she comes to Belvedere, where Jame Gumb lives, she finds an 'Orvieto of pigeon coops' behind the house where Frederica Bimmel lived. There are hundreds of pigeons there, feathers in the air and in the river. As she leaves, Mr Bimmel comes out with carcases. '"Squab", he said, when he saw Starling looking. "Ever eat squab?" "No," Starling said, turning back to the water. "I've eaten doves."'

It's an ominous remark, given that she has already been associated with Christ, when Lecter draws her face on his 'crucifixion watch'. Later, in *Hannibal*, there is a curious incident when Barney moves a dead pigeon being mourned by its mate. Lecter, too, offers a definition of Clarice as a 'deep-roller pigeon'.

There's also Jame Gumb's spaniel, Precious, used by Catherine Martin to save her skin. Precious is an allusion himself. In Titian's great painting *The Flaying of Marsyas*, which Dr Lecter commends to Clarice, just such a little dog is to be seen in the foreground – wagging its tail as it laps up the flayed faun's blood.

Most of the animal references in *The Silence of the Lambs* operate at the level of imagery, however. Again and again, people are compared to animal life. It has a powerful cumulative effect in drawing a picture of life in which animal imperatives operate, rather than any more elevated sense of what it is to be human. Harris's use of metaphor is not vague or suggestive. It's always cuttingly precise.

There are far too many such images to detail. A few?

Early on Graham warns Clarice to be careful of Lecter finding out about her: 'It's the kind of curiosity that makes a snake look in a bird's nest.' Lecter is the serpent to be sure, but Starling is the bird too. When Chilton shows Clarice his horrific photograph of one of Lecter's victims and watches her response, she thinks of 'a thirsty chicken pecking tears off her face'. Watching Senator Martin on television, Clarice is 'trembling like a terrier'. When Lecter shows Clarice the rhythm of Sammie's poem, 'Sammie's voice boomed behind her sudden as a leopard's cough, louder than a howler monkey'. Catherine Martin's fear stands on her chest 'the way a trapper kills a fox'. Jame Gumb's night sights 'look like crab eyes on stalks'; Catherine Martin curls up 'like a shrimp'. Clarice sizes up Catherine Martin's possessions 'intent as a lizard'. Looking at Lecter in Memphis, Clarice sees he is 'a cemetery mink'. Attacking the officers, Lecter is 'fast as a snapping turtle', he shakes his head 'like a rat-killing dog'. Even Ardelia Mapp has her predatory comparison: 'She could spot a test question in a lecture further than a leopard can see a limp'.

One of the effects of all this imagery of predation is to remind us that the forces of good here have within them possibilities of harm. 'Crawford's tired face was as sensitive to signals as the dished ruff of an owl and as free of mercy'. Later, we see the owlet moth in the Smithsonian. 'Pilcher blew air at it and instantly the fierce face of an owl appeared as the moth flared the undersides of its wings at them, the eye-spots on the wings glaring like the last sight a rat ever sees.'

Perhaps the most startling and poignant of all the natural images in *The Silence of the Lambs*, though, is the sentence describing dawn in the maximum security ward in the Hospital for the Criminally Insane: 'Down where it was never dark the tormented sense beginning day as oysters in a barrel open to their lost tide.' Just as he places his people firmly within the food chain, so too Harris puts them in a cosmological frame. Crawford after his wife has died: 'His empty hands hanging palms forward at his sides, he stood at the window looking to the empty east. He did not look for dawn; east was the only way the window faced.' See how well these sentences shape Crawford's plight, the pattern it makes of them.

Dr Lecter signs off in *The Silence of the Lambs*:

Orion is above the horizon now, and near it Jupiter, brighter than it will ever be again before the year 2000. (I have no intention of telling you the time and how high it is.) But I expect you can see it too. Some of our stars are the same.

Clarice.

Hannibal Lecter.

Far to the east, on the Chesapeake shore, Orion stood high in the clear night...

In *Hannibal*, Lecter flies back to America through the same constellation. 'We can see it through the vapour of our breath – in the clear night over Newfoundland a brilliant point of light hanging in Orion, then passing slowly overhead, a Boeing 747 bucking a hundred-mile-per-hour headwind westward.'

Orion is the sign of the hunter. Lecter and Clarice have this in common. When, looking into Frederica Bimmel's closet, Clarice suddenly realises what Jame Gumb is doing with the girls he is abducting, she has a moment of ecstasy. 'Starling put her head back, closed her eyes for one second. Problem-solving is hunting; it is savage pleasure and we are born to it.' In *Hannibal*, Rinaldo Pazzi has the same realisation, when he catches 'Il Mostro' by making the connection with Botticelli's *Primavera*: 'In that moment when the connection is made, in that synaptic spasm of completion when the thought drives through the red fuse, is our keenest pleasure. Rinaldo Pazzi had had the best moment of his life.'

Harris offers his readers the pleasures of problem-solving and making connections, of hunting. He takes pleasure himself in discovering these patterns and then making a world of them. Truly, he is a thriller writer.

Eight: Later Life

Thomas Harris's daily life, since his success gave him his independence, has been kept as private as he knows how. He makes no public appearances and he simply refuses to perform for the media, as most writers who hope to sell books must. His acquaintances have said remarkably little about him as well. No one who has his trust will talk about him. Those who do, by definition don't. That his friends have so thoroughly refused the journalists itself says most about him.

What little they do say about his character is consistent enough. Carole Baron, his long-term American editor, has said: 'He's private and ultimately very shy.' Another person who has dealt with him says: 'He's a wonderful client and a really nice guy but he's really not interested in appearing in the media. He leads a normal life and he's friends with all his publishers. He's very amicable, but he really doesn't like the media.' We noticed. Helen Fraser, his former editor at Heinemann, has said just a little more: 'Thomas is private to an excessive degree. He's big and round, very Southern and has a wonderful Mississippi accent. He's an absolutely delightful man, one of the nicest and warmest I've met. Southerners can be very deceptive though – he is very easygoing but underneath there might be something different.'

Harris has lived for some 20 years now with a former publishing editor, Pace Barnes, who has lately been head of publications for the Historical Society in Sag Harbor. His daughter, Anne, works in his publishing house in New York. She has plainly absorbed the *omertà* ethic too. 'I can only tell you I'm very proud of him and he works very hard,' she told Phoebe Hoban in 1991. Only his mother, Polly, of his close family, has been more talkative. She has said: 'I'm fed up with hearing that he's some weird recluse. He's not. He and Pace have a very nice life. They have a close circle of friends and they entertain regularly. But Tom never wanted to be a media celebrity. That's been the thing that has driven people crazy. He doesn't seek publicity. And people can't understand why not.'

Contrary to legend, mothers don't always know best. His uncle, James Arch Coleman, says: 'Tom is very private about what he does. He doesn't even tell his mother about what he's doing.' Who does?

The Harris family no longer have a property in

Rich, a neighbour confirms. Harris now lives in two popular resorts, Miami and Sag Harbor in the Hamptons, both a long way in every sense from the Delta. In both locations, Harris keeps a separate office as well as a home.

He moved first to Sag Harbor. In recent years, the Hamptons, on the eastern tip of Long Island, have become a great resort of the rich and famous. Summer residents include Martha Stewart, Paul Simon, Kim Basinger, Cindy Crawford, Martin Amis, Kurt Vonnegut, E.L. Doctorow, Calvin Klein, Ralph Lauren, Salman Rushdie, Estée Lauder, Donna Karan, Ben Bradlee, and recently the rap star Sean 'Puff Daddy' Combs.

There are long golden beaches, pleasant breezes, violet sunsets and three-star restaurants, just two hours from Wall Street. Steve Gaines, the author of *Philistines at the Hedgerow*, a social history of the Hamptons, says 'It's now easier to buy a $12,000 watch here than it is to buy a Coke.'

East Hampton is the glitziest village; Sag Harbor is 'the writers' Hampton'. Joel Aschenbach of the *Washington Post* went looking for Harris there and learned that he walks to the grocery store every morning and eats frequently at the best restaurant in the village, in the American Hotel, renovated in the early 1970s by a man who is now his friend, Ted Conklin. Wilfred Sheed, a writer and also a friend of Harris's, a little unkindly said: 'The tragedy of Tom's life is that he has a wonderful palate. He loves to eat, but he also has to diet.' He thought it 'the major tension in Harris's life'.

At six foot two, Harris is certainly large all round. The London tabloid the *Daily Star* once printed the picture of him with his spaniel with the *National Tattler*-worthy caption: '*Hannibal* author Thomas Harris, above, is a Captain Bird's Eye look-alike who is one of the top-selling authors of all time.' What more could we want to know?

In *Hannibal*, we notice that Dr Lecter is wistfully said to be 'imperially slim' and to move like a dancer. Anthony Hopkins failed to match this enviable state in the movie. These days Hopkins is just plain emperor-sized. It is part of Hannibal's supernaturalism that he is so strong, so lithe and so slender so late in life, without putting any work into it, whereas Barney, Margot and Francis Dolarhyde all need to work out. Harris, naturally, is a great noticer of weight and physique, as we all are. The topic is significant in *The Silence of the Lambs* in which Jame Gumb eats disgustingly. 'Jame Gumb took three TV dinners from his microwave oven. There were two Hungry Man dinners for himself and one Lean Cuisine for the poodle.' At six foot one, aged 34, he weighs 205 pounds (14 stone 9lb). As a result all his victims, chosen to fit, are 'heavy... large... big through the hips. Roomy', as lithe Hannibal and athletic Clarice progressively put it.

Clarice investigates the wardrobes of both Catherine Martin and Frederica Bimmel with understanding and sorrow. Catherine has clothes in two sizes, 'made to fit her at about 145 and 165 pounds, Starling guessed, and there were a few pairs of crisis fat pants and pullovers from the Statuesque Shop'. She finds many more signs of distress in Frederica Bimmel's room. 'Here were a couple of diet plans, the Fruit Juice Diet, the Rice Diet, and a crackpot plan where you don't eat and drink at the same sitting.' There are copies of a magazine called *Big Beautiful Girl* – and Starling spots that both girls have fat pants made by 'Juno'. 'Juno was a common brand, sold in a lot of places that handle outsizes, but it raised the question of clothing.' It sets off the train of thought that leads her to Gumb. In one of Harris's arabesques, the word has already been floated, when Crawford writes a small ad designed to lure the killer: 'Junoesque creamy passion flower, 21, model, seeks man who appreciates quality AND quantity', and then scratches out the 'Junoesque' and substitutes 'full-figured'.

Everybody refers to Harris's love of cooking and eating. His friend, the playwright Lanford Wilson, said: 'We write about what we know. He likes to eat. He likes to cook. He knows food.' There's an early indication of this in *Black Sunday*, where, to illustrate the passionlessness of Rachel Bauman's life in America, it is said out of nowhere that she eats 'dinners in smart and hollow places, where the chefs put coy signatures of garnishment on uninspired dishes'.

Phoebe Honan reported that Thomas Harris particularly liked preparing wild duck and venison. Perhaps, with one notable exception, the tastes he has given to Hannibal are his own? Dr Lecter favours foie gras, white truffles, figs, quail, partridge and green oysters from the Gironde (served to Starling Bordelaise style with a morsel of sausage). He drinks Bâtard-Montrachet, Yquem, Pétrus, a St-Estèphe and the Bordeaux aperitif Lillet. But perhaps not. These are grand items. Not being a realistic writer, writing moreover for a mass market, Harris has chosen just a few trophy dishes here. But Lecter does take his tastes seriously. Unmoved by attempts on his life, he is anxious about the best time to open and decant his Pétrus. 'This was what Dr Lecter considered a serious risk, more of a chance than he liked to take.'

Both Lecter and his creator love fast cars too. This is

a taste Harris has been able to share quite extensively with his characters. (When Clarice is attempting to pursue Lecter through his tastes, cars are the only area in which she feels confident.) Both of Clarice Starling's cars – a Pinto and a Mustang – are named after horses, and thus allude back to Hannah, the horse she saved as a child. Lecter escapes from Muskrat Farm in the Mustang: 'The guard at the main gatehouse looked up from his newspaper toward a distant sound, a ripping noise like a piston-engined fighter on a strafing run. It was a 5.0 litre Mustang turning 5800rpm across the interstate overpass.' Anybody who has ever heard a Spitfire or Hurricane make a pass will respond to that.

In Italy, Harris is reported to have driven an Alfa Romeo – the car which Pazzi, the Florentine detective, has commandeered from an imprisoned bank robber. Elsewhere he favours Jaguars, as does Lecter – after his escape, having driven before his arrest and his need for discretion, 'a supercharged Bentley'. The film critic David Thomson met Harris in 1992 at a dinner-party in Miami and noticed 'the obvious reverence he felt for another guest at our gathering Emerson Fittipaldi, the motor-racing driver'.

Then again, it's reported that Harris likes drawing and once, as a joke, submitted his work to an exhibition of 'outsider art'. Lecter loves to draw. In his cell, Clarice sees his view of Florence, drawn from memory, and of Golgotha after the Deposition, the central Cross empty, Christ having vacated the world. He sketches each of his own hands ambidextrously with the other, and he catches Clarice. 'Indulge me a moment, Clarice. Would you let your head hang forward, just let it hang forward as if you were asleep. A second more. Thank you, I've got it now.' She sees the result in his patent application for his 'crucifixion watch'.

Harris also likes to travel to Europe, especially Italy and France. He is reported to spend some time in Paris each year and to have attended the Cordon Bleu school there. His attachment to Italy is unmistakable in *Hannibal* too. When *Red Dragon* appeared in 1981, the book jacket stated 'at present he lives in Italy'.

There has been the odd sighting over the years. In 1994, he attended the trial in Italy of Pietro Pacciani, 'Il Mostro', the Monster of Florence, taking his own longhand notes. For 30 years, Florence had been terrorised by the murder of courting couples. In 1986, the investigation was taken over by Ruggiero Perugini, an Italian who had worked in the FBI. Perugini used computer analysis to reduce the list of suspects to ten. (The equivalent detective in *Hannibal* is Rinaldo Pazzi, a 'Pazzi of the Pazzi' and a patsy.)

In 1993, as a result of Perugini's initiatives, Pietro

Pacciani – a semi-literate labourer, who had previously served 13 years for murdering a man he saw with his fiancée, and another sentence for sexually abusing his daughters – was arrested. In 1995, Pacciani was convicted of seven double murders. He continued to maintain that he was a lamb not a wolf, 'as innocent as Christ on the Cross'. In February 1996 an appeals court overturned his conviction on a technicality and he was set free. In December 1996, a retrial was ordered as it became apparent that Pacciani may have been part of a gang. The trial of the accomplices began in 1997. On 22 February 1998, Pacciani, then 73, was found dead in his home in odd circumstances, with his face distorted, his trousers down and shirt pulled up. It was concluded he had died of a heart attack. Some believe him to have been murdered by the real Mostro. These events have some bearing on the first part of *Hannibal* and the date of its composition.

Back in the United States, Harris has continued to sit in on police training courses and conferences up to quite a recent date. There's one in Orlando for homicide detectives and forensic experts which he attended for three years running in the 1990s. These trained observers came up with the following observations for the reporter Meg Laughlin: ' "He really likes to have a few drinks with us at the end of the day," said

Dave Rivers, a retired Miami homicide cop. "He listened for hours while I told him what a crime scene says about a serial killer," said Kentucky forensic profiler Ron Holmes. "I never saw him look happier than when he was eating a good fish sandwich," said North Carolina police academy instructor Don Raymond.' It's just possible that Harris noticed more about these detectives than they did about him, as he's been doing for years.

For all the slowness with which he publishes, it seems that Harris's working habits are regular. 'He is a creature of habit,' says Mom. In Sag Harbor, he used to rent a room over Marty's barbershop in Main Street. In Miami, he has another office a couple of miles from his home, in a residential block with no phone or fax. 'While finishing the book [*Hannibal*] in Miami, he left home every morning at precisely nine am and drove 2.1 miles to his office, following the same route every day', Caroline Graham reported, reverently.

By all accounts, what then happens in that office is not a spontaneous overflow. Nikkie Finke, the Hollywood correspondent for *Salon*, quotes (without attribution) a reply that Harris once gave to somebody who asked him why the sequel to *The Silence of the Lambs* was taking so long: 'Let me tell you about my day. I get up at eight in the morning. I leave the house at 8.30 and

I arrive in my office at 8.36. I stay in the office until two in the afternoon. And between 8.37 am and 2pm, I'm doing one of three things. I'm writing; I'm staring out the window; or I' m writhing on the floor.'

One of Harris's friends, the playwright Joe Pintauro, reported much the same lack of enthusiasm. 'We were talking about writing. Tom was telling me, "I'd rather dig a ditch 60 feet long than do one day's work of writing. That is how it feels to me. It is very difficult."' He is still a country boy, the comparison shows.

As we know, it took Thomas Harris six years to write *Red Dragon*, seven years to write *The Silence of the Lambs*, 11 years to write Hannibal. On this scale of progress, he might deliver his next book in about 2014, a year we haven't yet got comfortable about pronouncing. Or he may just surprise us.

There were special problems about *Hannibal*, we can surmise. In 1991, the film of *The Silence of the Lambs* appeared and Hannibal Lecter became public property on a different scale. Lecter was out, and in some ways out of Harris's control too. There's some controversy over whether he even saw the film. He had, it appears, not much liked *Manhunter*, in which Brian Cox plays Lecter. 'He didn't think they did it any justice', reported his uncle. *Manhunter* took only $8.5

million at the box office – and *Red Dragon* may yet be remade. Cox did not make his Lecter alluring as Hopkins was to do. 'I was interested in that childlike immorality he had. And while a lot of people get off on him, I never imagined him as the heroic figure he became. I still have a problem with that,' Cox said.

The Silence of the Lambs, however, definitively gave Lecter a face and a voice. The image created by Anthony Hopkins has overtaken the author's own conception. A number of those close to Harris have insisted that he tried to protect himself from this effect by never seeing the film. His agent Mort Janklow says so. 'He has never seen *Silence of the Lambs*, quite deliberately. He'd love to see it, but it would impinge on his own vision.' Carole Baron (his editor) thinks the same. 'He was thrilled with the Academy Awards it won, but since the characters came from his own mind, he didn't want to be influenced by the movie.'

John Douglas is sure he never saw it too. 'It was a little different from his book and he didn't want to be swayed by the way it ended in case it affected his next book. Before *The Silence of the Lambs* was released, he was watching a movie when a trailer for *Silence* came on. He got up and walked right out of the theatre.'

Mom again knows different. 'I've read that Tom's never seen the film. Of course he has. He told me he would love Anthony Hopkins to play Hannibal again,' she said, before the making of *Hannibal*. Harris has also offered a few remarks that might suggest he did see the film, so polite are they. He told Phoebe Hoban: 'It's a great movie. I've been surrounded by it, so I wanted to see it. I admire Jonathan Demme, and we were very fortunate to have him and [screenwriter] Ted Tally, and we were very lucky with the cast.' Which, read carefully, doesn't confirm that he actually did see it.

Either way, Harris must have become aware of the way the audience was making Hannibal Lecter into a form of hero. David Thomson, the film critic, met Harris in Miami after the movie had been out for a year and formed the impression that 'the success of *Lambs*, and above all the triumph of Hopkins (and the way Lecter had become a household name), had surprised him and altered his sense of his own character. For whereas Harris had set out to describe an evil, dangerous man, he found that his own creation had, somehow, swelled with charm – or our affection.' Thomson put this down to the fact that moral judgement is possible in literature but in all forms of theatre, and especially in the movies, actors inevitably try to make their characters appealing, seductive. Hannibal certainly became a hero to many who had had their ideas formed more by the film than the book, as grotesque websites called Loving Lecter and Lecterphilia show. One of these sites specialises in amateur Lecter fiction – as though he were a generally available stereotype or mythological figure.

Yet Harris remained the only one with access to the fictional world he had created and for 11 years there was not a word from him. His situation, perhaps, was comparable only to that of Sir Arthur Conan Doyle after he had thrown Sherlock Holmes down the Reichenbach Falls. The death of Sherlock Holmes was announced in the *Strand Magazine* for Christmas 1893. In 1896, Conan Doyle told the Authors' Club: 'I hold that it was not murder, but justifiable homicide in self-defence, since, if I had not killed him, he would certainly have killed me.' But after ten years (in which he had written the prequel, *The Hound of the Baskervilles*, 1902), he consented to *The Return of Sherlock Holmes* (*Collier's Magazine*, October 1903).

Conan Doyle spoke of Holmes just as Harris does of Lecter, indeed so similarly that Harris may have modelled his manner on Conan Doyle's. Conan Doyle, 1904: 'So far as I know there is not the slightest intention of his ever again entering on the work of the detection of crime... From what I know, Sherlock Holmes's retirement will be final. He will not again emerge.' Thomas Harris, 1991: 'People ask me if he's coming back but I don't know, he doesn't return my phone calls. He's a man who has to amuse himself...'

Dr Lecter did come back. On 21 March 1999, Harris posted copies of a 600-page typescript from Miami to his agent Mort Janklow and to his editor Carole Baron in New York. They arrived two days later. On 30 March, the *New York Times* announced the news: 'Long after *Lambs*, Dr Lecter is Returning'. The book was rushed into print and published on both sides of the Atlantic on 8 June. That evening, Harris attended a small cocktail party held by his publisher in New York. 'He was very gracious and thanked everybody,' says Carole Baron. With Baron, Janklow, and their spouses, his daughter and his partner Pace Barnes, Harris went out to dinner that night at Le Cirque. 'And then he disappeared. His duties are over.'

Nine: Hannibal

Hannibal, so long awaited, rapidly disappointed and affronted many of its readers. It has the distinction of having, among its more than 2,500 reader-reviews on Amazon.com, nearly 700 which give it the lowest possible rating. 'Even fans should be disgusted by his laziness'; 'This book is horrible'; 'This really sucked';

'Depressingly awful'; 'MADE ME VOMIT'; 'Boring'; 'Absolutely ridiculous'; 'A weak and gory novel' – on they go, not all of them misspelt either.

The most forcefully negative review was published by Martin Amis in *Talk* magazine. Amis had previously admired Harris's books and still does admire *Red Dragon* and *The Silence of the Lambs*. 'In these books Harris has done what all popular writers hope to do: he has created a parallel world, a terrible antiterra, airless and arcane but internally coherent. It is the world of the human raptor in the American setting (with his equipment, his weapons, his mobility), and of those who would hunt him down. Harris's subject is predacity – serial murder – but his intelligent eye is alert to its quieter manifestations.'

But Amis went to town on *Hannibal*, calling it 'on all levels, a snorting, rooting, oinking porker, complete with twinkling trotters and twirlaround tail'. He proclaimed it: 'helplessly *voulu*, sentimental and corrupt'.

The problem, Amis found, was that Harris had 'gone gay' for Hannibal and 'palpably wearied of Clarice'. He objected to the back story given for Hannibal's childhood and he called the book's climax 'a riot of paceless implausibilities'. He scoffed at the snobbish tastes of Lecter and the hokey nastiness of

Mason Verger. He didn't care for the style too much either. 'Needless to say, Harris has become a serial murderer of English sentences, and *Hannibal* is a necropolis of prose. With the change of genre, from procedural thriller to Gothic fantasy, all internal coherence is lost.' Definitely, he didn't like it. Another factor was at work, too. Amis had been much antagonised by reviewers who, by promoting the genre novelist, contrived to 'demote his mainstream counterpart' – modestly mentioning no names.

That fine genre novelist, Stephen King, was more generous. Writing in the *New York Times*, he actually rated *Hannibal* more highly than the previous Lecter novels. 'Sequels are usually lame ducks, poor things that are unable to keep up with their predecessors. *Hannibal* is really not a sequel at all, but rather the third and most satisfying part of one very long and scary ride through the haunted palace of abnormal psychiatry.' He emphasised that Hannibal is 'a full-out, unabashed horror novel'. '*Hannibal* is a balloon Harris bats steadily onward, probably with a grin on his face. The balloon happens to be full of poison gas and bad dreams, true... but Harris is not writing for everyone. This is authentic witch's brew, eye of newt and haunch of redneck, not chicken soup.'

King's appreciation of Hannibal was heightened by

his own understanding of the difficulty of such writing. 'No character in popular fiction is as fragile as the monster, or so prone to losing his pants in his later appearances.' For all his admiration, he suggested that Harris would do well to 'bar this door and go down a different corridor' for his next book. 'Familiarity, even with a monster, breeds contempt.'

Hannibal is indeed different from its predecessors. Harris has changed genre here and he has changed his characters too. Many readers have felt these changes to be tantamount to an act of aggression against them. They are correct about that. Harris has exerted his authorial right to take his story where his readers may not want it to go.

The events of *Hannibal* are simply enough told. (Stop right here if you haven't read it yet and still plan to do so. Here.) It opens with a shoot-out, as though to leave behind the genre of the procedural novel with a bang. Clarice Starling goes on a botched drugs raid with her old comrade in arms, John Brigham. He dies and she survives by killing five people, including a mother carrying her child. The carnage is filmed by a tipped-off news crew (Harris hasn't eased up on the media) and Starling is in disgrace. Her old enemy in the FBI, Krendler, plans to take this opportunity to destroy her career.

Seven years have passed since Lecter's escape with no word from him. Now another letter arrives from him to Clarice, in response to her disgrace. It is a message of encouragement: 'You are a warrior, Clarice.' She is given a respite from ruin by being put on the case to find Lecter.

We are introduced to the villain of the book: Mason Verger. Verger is a paedophile, a sadist, a murderer and a keen Christian. He is also a physical wreck, having been one of Dr Lecter's early victims. Verger is on a respirator, paralysed save for one arm. He has just the one eye and no face, having, under Lecter's influence, cut it all off with a piece of glass and fed it to his dogs. In his room, 'it is dark except for the glow of the big aquarium where an exotic eel turns and turns in an endless figure of eight... "Its common name is the Brutal Moray, would you like to see why?"' He has a sister, Margot, a lesbian bodybuilder whom he abused as a child but who is now co-operating with him in the hope of extracting some sperm from him to carry on the Verger line.

Mason Verger is the heir to a meatpacking fortune and he is using his money to take appropriate revenge on Lecter. Not only has he posted a reward on Lecter, he has also suborned various members of the FBI to work on his behalf. Verger intends to have Lecter fed alive, feet first, to a herd of specially bred carnivorous pigs.

We move to Florence. Rinaldo Pazzi, a detective from an old Florentine family, is in disgrace too. His triumph in the case of the serial killer 'Il Mostro' has unravelled into disaster. Then he discovers that a scholar living in Florence under the name of 'Dr Fell' is the fugitive Hannibal Lecter. Instead of notifying the authorities, Pazzi decides to sell Lecter alive to Mason Verger.

The first attempt to seize Lecter by Verger's men fails. After having delivered a lecture in the Palazzo Vecchio on avarice, hanging and self-destruction, Lecter murders Pazzi by hanging him out of the window, eviscerated, just as Pazzi's ancestor was executed in the 15th century. Then Lecter flees Italy and returns to America. He assumes a new identity and settles in, taking up his old pursuits: the arts, gastronomy and predation.

Meanwhile, back at Quantico, Clarice Starling has begun 'to pursue Dr Lecter down the corridors of his taste', by setting up computer traces on the sales of the things she knows he favours. 'Taste. The wine, the truffles. Taste in all things was a constant between Dr Lecter's lives in America and Europe, between his life as a successful medical practitioner and fugitive monster.

His face may have changed but his tastes did not, and he was not a man who denied himself.'

Her researches will lead eventually to Lecter's detection. But she is unaware that all her work is on behalf of Mason Verger, rather than the FBI, for Verger has put her superior, Deputy Assistant Inspector General Paul Krendler, on his payroll. In his efforts to track down Lecter, Verger also consults a psychologist – Dr Doemling from Baylor University – and hires Barney, the warder who used to guard him in the Hospital for the Criminally Insane. As Starling gets nearer to finding Lecter, Krendler has her suspended from the Bureau, so that he can be the one to deliver Lecter to Verger. Starling loses all faith in the forces of law and order. Her mentor Jack Crawford, unable to protect her, collapses with a heart attack.

Lecter is finally abducted by Verger's men as he attempts to leave Starling a birthday present. Preparations are made to feed him to the herd of savage pigs, flown over from Sardinia for the purpose. But just as this grotesque vengeance is about to proceed, Clarice Starling, once again acting all alone, intervenes. She rescues Lecter but in the process is hit with darts from a tranquilliser gun and loses consciousness. Lecter carries her off to his hideaway. Back at the ranch, Margot Verger murders her brother Mason, after extracting the sperm she wants with a cattle prod, by putting the moray eel down his throat, conveniently blaming Lecter.

In his *soigné* residence, Dr Lecter tends Clarice Starling, using hypnotism and mind-altering drugs to bend her to his will. To strip away her last loyalties and inhibitions, he shows her the bones of her beloved father, which he has collected from a Texas cemetery. 'This is what he is, this is all of him now. This is what time has reduced him to.'

Then Lecter kidnaps Krendler, removes the top half of his skull and brings him, tethered, sedated but still conscious and talkative, to his elegantly decorated dinner-table. Carefully he prepares a *beurre noisette* sauce, with shallots, capers and truffles, and then slices off portions of Krendler's brain to serve to Clarice, lightly sautéed.

'How is it?' Krendler asked, once again behind the flowers and speaking immoderately loud, as persons with lobotomies are prone to do.

'Really excellent,' Starling said. 'I've never had caper berries before.'

Krendler becomes abusive.

'You could never answer the phone in my office. You

sound like a cornbread country cunt,' Krendler yelled through the flowers.

'See if I sound like Oliver Twist when I ask for MORE,' Starling replied, releasing in Dr Lecter glee he could scarcely contain.

Krendler's brain is reduced 'back nearly to the premotor cortex'. Hannibal and Clarice become lovers. The doctor, late in life, has met his match.

At this point, Clarice is still drugged and perhaps a little hypnotised and it remains uncertain whether or not Lecter means to let her live. In a brief coda, however, we are shown them happily co-habiting in Buenos Aires three years later. They go to the opera, they travel by Mercedes Maybach, they speak foreign languages together, they dance and they have great sex. 'Sex is a splendid structure they add to every day.'

The narrator warns us to leave them alone for our own safety. 'We'll withdraw now while they are dancing on the terrace... For either of them to discover us would be fatal. We can only learn so much and live.'

It will be seen from this plot summary that this is not a book that conforms with slavish exactitude to the tenets of socialist realism. It does not offer inspiring role models. Even those who, less demandingly, just like their fiction to be about people like them, doing the kinds of things they might do, will be unimpressed by *Hannibal*. They'll spot it at once as far-fetched and, soon after, as nasty and ridiculous. In due course, they will proceed under their own steam to declare it offensive. Let us bid them farewell.

Let's admit too that *Hannibal* is an imperfect book, compared with the taut machine that is *The Silence of the Lambs*. It shows the traces of having been worked on over a period of time with the different layers never being wholly integrated. It is neither as suspenseful nor as genuinely frightening as its predecessors. There are even *longueurs*. Yet it is, in its own way, like no other novel whatsoever, a masterpiece.

The one mistake in judgment, which even its admirers may concede, is that Hannibal Lecter is provided, in flashback, with a childhood that goes some way to explaining his nature. In 1944, after the collapse of the Eastern Front, his parents are killed on the family estate in Lithuania. It is taken over by 'a mixed bag of deserters', perhaps Nazis. Lecter, aged six, sees them slaughter a deer for food, so explaining his antagonism to deer hunters. Then the deserters come for a child and take his sister, Mischa, aged four.

He prayed so hard that he would see Mischa again, the prayer consumed his six-year-old mind, but it did not drown out the sound of the axe. His prayer to see her again did not go entirely unanswered – he did see a few of Mischa's milk teeth in the reeking stool pit his captors used...

Since this partial answer to his prayers, Hannibal Lecter had not been bothered by any considerations of deity, other than to recognise how his own modest predations paled beside those of God, who is in irony matchless, and in wanton malice beyond measure.

This passage – although illuminatingly establishing that in this world God is to be seen as just the biggest predator of all, at the very top of the food chain – has been much reviled. 'That will cut you some slack, won't it, having your little sister eaten by Nazis?' jeered Martin Amis. It has been noted that it directly contradicts Lecter's fierce speech to Clarice, in *The Silence of the Lambs*, on their first meeting, when she suggests he might be curious about what happened to him.

'Nothing happened to me, Officer Starling. I happened. You can't reduce me to a set of influences. You've given up good and evil for behaviourism, Officer Starling. You've got everybody in moral dignity pants – nothing is ever anybody's fault. Look at me, Officer Starling. Can you stand to say I'm evil? Am I evil, Officer Starling?'

It's been objected that equipping Lecter with a tormented childhood like this makes him less remarkable. It reduces his charisma. But Harris has always chosen to describe the childhoods of his murderers. As a novelist, he firmly believes us to be not only born but made. Lecter, in manipulating Clarice Starling at the end of the book, relies upon this too: 'Ever, Dr Lecter sought pattern. He knew that, like every sentient being, Starling formed from her early experience matrices, frameworks by which later perceptions were understood.' In return, it may well save Clarice Starling's life, at the end of her dinner with Dr Lecter, that she, too, sees a matrix in Lecter's mind – and offers him her breast, dripping not with milk but warmed Yquem.

It is hardly imaginable that having at last come to the fore, as a free agent, in a novel of this length, that Lecter should not have some motivation given. The angry response of so many readers shows how much they themselves had had invested in the idea of Lecter as glamorously inexplicable, thrillingly pure in his evil.

One of the difficult things Harris does in *Hannibal* is quite deliberately to take back his character from the public who had so fecklessly embraced him. The scene announcing this comes early in the section set in Florence – the chapters about the exhibition of Atrocious Torture Instruments, which Lecter attends repeatedly, to look at the spectators not at the displays.

The passage opens with one of the oracular apho-risms that stand free from the flow of the narrative in *Hannibal* and show how far back from the scene of the action the text is being delivered. 'Now that ceaseless exposure has calloused us to the lewd and the vulgar, it is instructive to see what still seems wicked to us. What still slaps the clammy flab of our submissive consciousness hard enough to get our attention?' One obvious answer: the figure of Hannibal Lecter himself. That's the aggression of the author here against his own readers. As John Lanchester noted in his thoughtful review of *Hannibal*: 'He is attractive because we are repulsive; the more people like Lecter, the worse the news about human nature.'

A page later comes the equally ferocious statement already quoted in the discussion of the Baudelaire poem, 'Au Lecteur': 'The essence of the worst, the true asafoetida of the human spirit, is not found in the Iron Maiden or the whetted edge; Elemental Ugliness is found in the faces of the crowd.' Not in Lecter – in you, hypocrite *lecteur*.

If many of Harris's fans have been choked at Lecter's development in *Hannibal*, still more have refused to swallow what happens to Clarice Starling, becoming Lecter's lover, turning murderer and cannibal

– never mind that it was so carefully prognosticated in *The Silence of the Lambs*, her exchanges with Lecter having been a form of surrendering her soul to the devil in exchange for advancement. The turn of events still came as a complete shock to some, including Jodie Foster, it appears. Before she read the script she was saying, 'I have a real deep connection to Clarice and I feel that I know her the way I know my sister or my brother.' It's good to be careful who you call brother. She eventually pulled out, saying: 'It's not for me.' She did not like the way the story ended.

Nor did the eventual producers of the movie. Having paid so much for the rights, they eventually made a film of the novel they would have preferred Harris to have written, rather than the one he did. A first script by David Mamet sticking more closely to the book was trenchantly revised by Steve Zaillian. Much of the novel was just deleted. Such characters as Ardelia Mapp, Jack Crawford and Margot Verger were eliminated entirely. Other aspects were changed. Mason Verger was given back his mobility and a face of a kind, so as to have some cinematic presence. 'If I'd kept him lying there in a dark room, we might have run out of things to do; limited the actor,' said the director Ridley Scott.

But the central alteration was that Clarice Starling

is never seduced by Hannibal Lecter. Throughout the final scene she was made to struggle bravely, drugged and wounded as she was, to have him arrested. Although the film-makers had cheerfully retained all the gore, they had flunked the challenge of the moral horror.

An interview with the director, Ridley Scott, gave an interesting glimpse of Harris's attitude to the film and the cuts and changes that were required. Before beginning work, Scott called Harris to 'discuss which babies he was prepared to lose'. Harris told him: 'It's taken me nine years to get this book written. Just keep me in the picture.' Eventually, he spent five days with Scott and Zaillian discussing the script. Scott: 'He'd been nervous about our proposed ending. The book reached for something that was in his heart, obviously... Clarice goes off with Hannibal at the end of the book. I felt it was too much of a quantum leap that a straight arrow like Clarice would do such a thing... I came up with this alternative idea and Harris said, "I'd have to see it." So he saw it, and was gracious enough to say, "You're absolutely right."' There is the courteous Harris again, wishing them well. Whether he really felt he had got it wrong in those nine years and that the movie-makers had got it right in a few days is another matter entirely.

Let us cite here another of the oracular aphorisms that stud *Hannibal* like nails, the one introducing Pazzi's decision to sell Lecter: 'How do you behave when you know the conventional honours are dross? When you have come to believe with Marcus Aurelius that the opinion of future generations will be worth no more than the opinion of the current one? Is it possible to behave well then? Desirable to behave well then?' Well, reader?

One other aspect the movie got sorely wrong was the age of Clarice Starling. In the movie, Julianne Moore, who otherwise played her well enough, was 42 and a mother and she looked it. Nor was she any athlete. It matters. All of the climax of *Hannibal* is triggered by Lecter's gift. 'Her birthday was coming soon, the doctor reflected, He wondered if there was extant a bottle of Château d'Yquem from her birth year. Perhaps a present was in order for Clarice Starling, who in three weeks would have lived as long as Christ.' He is captured while delivering it on the eve (or perhaps the very day) of her 33rd birthday, near Christmas. Clarice has, of course, already been associated with Christ by Lecter – not least on the face of his 'crucifixion watch'.

Just like Francis Dolarhyde, a change has been triggered in her by her awareness of ageing. 'She was suddenly a thirty-three-year-old woman, alone, with a ruined civil service career and no shotgun, standing in a forest at night. She saw herself clearly, saw the crinkles of age beginning in the corner of her eyes.' ('*Nel mezzo del cammin di nostra vita/mi ritrovai per una selva oscura,/che la diritta via era smarrita.*')

There is a 'sea change' at work in Clarice Starling early on in *Hannibal*. She has lost faith in the Bureau, in 'technique'. She herself has commented to Crawford that Lecter wrote her a letter because: 'He thought what happened to me would... destroy, would disillusion me about the Bureau, and he enjoys seeing the destruction of faith, it's his favourite thing.' Lecter is right. Her faith has been destroyed.

'Having come to doubt the religion of technique, where could Starling turn? In her tribulation, in the gnawing sameness of her days, she began to look at the shape of things. She began to credit her own visceral reactions to things, without quantifying them or restricting them to words.'

She turns to taste. And taste isn't kind. It is taste that will lead her eventually to say to Lecter, just before they dine on Krendler: 'Damn a bunch of self-improvement. I want a pleasant dinner.'

The tempter has triumphed. Lecter anticipated Starling's progress years back in his prison cell, as Barney recalls. 'I can just repeat what he told me – he could see what she was becoming, she was charming the way a cub is charming, a small cub that will grow up to be – like one of the big cats. One you can't play with later. She had the cublike earnestness, he said. She had all the weapons, in miniature and growing, and all she knew so far was how to wrestle with the other cubs. That amused him.'

When she faces down Lecter before their dinner, he applies to her another comparison from nature harking back to the metamorphosis so craved by Jame Gumb. 'It occurred to Dr Lecter in the moment that with all his knowledge and intrusion, he could never entirely predict her, or own her at all. He could feed the caterpillar, he could whisper through the chrysalis; what hatched out followed its own nature and was beyond him. He wondered if she had the .45 on her leg beneath the gown.'

Having traced the prevalence of predatory creatures throughout Harris's work, the part played in *Hannibal* by the man-eating swine and the moray eel will not surprise us. To readers coming to him cold they may seem absurdly unwieldy devices, but *Hannibal* reaches to a form of poetry, rather than to the police procedural.

There is again an extraordinarily extensive animal symbolism at work, as well as all these animals functioning in the plot. Lecter is the snake, Krendler a hyena, Starling variously a dove and a deer. Mason Verger is a creature of the underworld, underwater. 'Mason Verger, noseless and lipless, with no soft tissue on his face, was all teeth, like a creature of the deep, deep ocean.' His single eye is 'ever open like the eyes of the great eel', his hand walks on its fingers over his sheets, 'like a crab'. When the eel kills him, it seizes his tongue 'with its razor-sharp teeth as it would a fish'.

Hannibal does depict the world as an Inferno. Lecter's Dante lecture, followed by his heavily symbolic murder of Pazzi, shows us that. So do the numerous casual references to Hell: 'If there are depots on the way to Hell, they must resemble the ambulance entrance to Maryland-Misericordia General Hospital.'

The novel deploys the method of Dante: the *contrapasso*, the punishment that is 'a sort of intensification or symbolic inversion of the dominant crime'. Such is the punishment that Verger intends to inflict on Lecter but suffers himself. There is a sustained blasphemy throughout *Hannibal*. It makes repeated Biblical allusions (as indeed it does to Classical and even Egyptian mythology). Mason Verger is an enthusiastic Christian on this principle: 'God's choices in inflicting suffering are not satisfactory to us, nor are they understandable, unless innocence offends Him. Clearly

He needs some help in directing the blind fury with which He flogs the earth.'

Verger had his epiphany at Christmas, listening to children singing carols. 'At Christmas communions around the earth, the devout believe that, through the miracle of transubstantiation, they eat the actual body and blood of Christ. Mason began the preparations for an even more impressive ceremony with no transub-stantiation necessary. He began his arrangements for Dr Hannibal Lecter to be eaten alive.' Mason tells Starling just what Christ means to him. ' "I'm free, Miss Starling, and it's all okay now. I'm right with Him and it's all okay now. He's the Risen Jesus, and at camp we called him the Riz. Nobody beats the Riz. We made it contemporary, you know, the Riz... He will raise me up from this bed and He will smite mine enemies and drive them before me and I will hear the lamentations of their women, and it's all okay now." He choked on saliva and stopped, the vessels on the front of his head dark and pulsing.'

The name for this is Southern Gothic. It's a product of the peculiar religious atmosphere of the Bible Belt, where fundamentalist Christianity is so omnipresent and unregulated that it gets used as a justification for all kinds of demented self-assertion, such as Verger's. This is Protestantism at its extreme: Verger believes that redeemed as he is, he can do as he likes. Lecter, on the other hand, believes that the worst he can do is nothing to what God can do in the way of predation.

Throughout, *Hannibal* is a landscape, like the South itself, shot through with the Bible, reduced to shreds. Harris, who plainly has seen much Bible-bashing, not least at Baylor, may be using it here for 'the theological hokum the Gothic novel requires', as one critic puts it. Yet all blasphemy depends upon the sacred against which to blaspheme.

There is one more quality about *Hannibal* to note. The writing is remarkable. Hannibal Lecter, following the wisdom of the ancients, has constructed a 'memory palace' in which he can dwell. 'The memory palace was a mnemonic system well known to ancient scholars and much information was preserved in them through the Dark Ages while Vandals burned the books. Like scholars before him, Dr Lecter stores an enormous amount of information keyed to objects in his thousand rooms, but, unlike the ancients, Dr Lecter has a second purpose for his palace; sometimes he lives there.'

According to the rules 'discovered by Simonides of Ceos and elaborated by Cicero 400 years later', the memory palace is 'airy, high-ceilinged, furnished with objects and tableaux that are vivid, striking, sometimes shocking and absurd, and often beautiful.'

Cicero (quoted by Frances A. Yates in *The Art of Memory*) urges us to devise always exceptional images. 'When we see in everyday life things that are petty, ordinary and banal, we generally fail to remember them, because the mind is not being stirred by anything novel or marvellous. But if we see or hear something exceptionally base, dishonourable, unusual, great, unbelievable, or ridiculous, that we are likely to remember for a long time.' Harris has a fantastic gift for saying the thing about a person or a situation that will tell all and fix it in the mind for ever. *Hannibal* is itself furnished with objects and tableaux that are vivid, striking, sometimes shocking and absurd, and often beautiful. *Hannibal* is itself a memory palace.

Ten: Gothic

How good, then, is Harris? Martin Amis, kicking *Hannibal*, complains about the 'levelling impulse' which would enlist him in the ranks of literature. He believes in 'the hierarchy of the talents'. Fine.

Let us say then that Thomas Harris writes melodrama, 'a dramatic piece characterised by sensational incident and violent appeals to the emotions', not high literature. But melodrama has its own long history, as T.S. Eliot emphasised in his essay distinguishing between the achievements of Wilkie Collins and Dickens (1927): 'Those who have lived before such terms as "high-brow fiction", "thrillers" and "detective fiction" were invented realise that melodrama is perennial and the craving for it is perennial and must be satisfied. If we cannot get this satisfaction out of what the publishers present as "literature" then we will read – with less and less pretence of concealment – what we call "thrillers". But in the golden age of melodramatic fiction there was no such distinction. The best novels were thrilling...' No longer. The pleasures Harris offers are not to be found in contemporary literary fiction, in Britain, certainly.

Thomas Harris easily stands comparison with the great melodramatists of the past: Bram Stoker, Conan Doyle, Wilkie Collins or Edgar Allan Poe, say, perhaps even Robert Louis Stevenson. He will last as they have lasted.

In his essay, T.S. Eliot compared Wilkie Collins's characters to those of Dickens: 'In comparison with the characters of Dickens they lack only that kind of reality which is almost supernatural, which hardly seems rather to descend upon him by a kind of inspiration or grace. Collins's best characters are fabricated with consummate skill, before our eyes; in Dickens's greatest figures we see no process of calculation. Dickens's figures belong to poetry, like figures of Dante or Shakespeare, in that a single phrase, either by them or about them, may be enough to set them wholly before us.' Only a deaf critic would deny that Thomas Harris has his phrases.

Another name for Thomas Harris's form of literature is Gothic. One of his more refined reviewers put it like this back in 1989 when *The Silence of the Lambs* was published in the UK: 'Gothic fiction, of which Mr Harris seems to me the finest living exponent in English, has always been puzzle-headed. It lives on the intellectual shadows which enlightened views cast; it is a sanctuary for stubborn inexplicables – how life comes to be, sexual attraction, willed cruelty – in a world of knowingness. The lurid events of such stories stand in exact relation to the fact that we do not know what to make of them, what they mean, for they are stories of our incapacity to understand what we at other times smoothly formulate.'

Specifically, Thomas Harris is an exponent of Southern Gothic, or the Grotesque. The stories we know as *Tales of Mystery and Imagination*, Edgar Allan Poe originally called 'Tales of the Grotesque and Arabesque', a term that will do well enough for Harris.

Some Southern writers have complained about the use of this term. Flannery O'Connor said in 1963:

'We're all grotesque and I don't think the Southerner is any more grotesque than anyone else; but his social situation demands more of him than that elsewhere in this country. It requires considerable grace for two races to live together, particularly when the population is divided about 50–50 between them and when they have our particular history. It can't be done without a code of manners based on mutual charity... After the Civil War, formality became a condition of survival... In practice, the Southerner seldom underestimates his own capacity for evil.'

O'Connor complained a little about the image the Southern school of writers had – 'often the term conjures up an image of Gothic monstrosities and the idea of a preoccupation with everything deformed and grotesque'. It does still. On the excellent website Hanno-tations, there is this sublime definition from a Southern writer, Pat Conroy: 'My mother, Southern to the bone, once told me, "All Southern literature can be summed up in these words: *On the night the hogs ate Willie, Mama died when she heard what Daddy did to Sister.*" '

But O'Connor also argued in an essay called 'The Grotesque in Southern Fiction' for the strengths of the genre, in words that can be applied directly to Thomas Harris: 'In these grotesque works, we find that the writer has made alive some experience which we are not accustomed to observe every day, or which the ordinary man may never experience in his ordinary life. We find connections which we would expect in the customary kind of realism have been ignored, that there are strange skips and gaps which anyone trying to describe manners and customs would certainly not have left. Yet the characters have an inner coherence, if not always a coherence to their social framework. Their fictional qualities lean away from typical social patterns, towards mystery and the unexpected.'

Such work should not be downgraded in the name of supposedly more realistic fiction, she insisted. 'The writer who writes within what might be called the modern romance tradition may not be writing novels which in all respects partake of a novelistic orthodoxy; but as long as these works have vitality, as long as they present something that is alive, however eccentric its life may seem to the general reader, then they have to be dealt with; and they have to be dealt with on their own terms.'

Thomas Harris's romances have such life and they set their own terms. They have their place in the literature of our time. For, as T.S. Eliot said, 'so long as novels are written, the possibilities of melodrama must from time to time be re-explored'. That is what Thomas Harris is doing for us. And this achievement began in the flat fields and the baking heat of the Mississippi Delta, where the blues were born – and where the young Thomas Harris first began to take an interest in the way one animal preys upon another.

SELECTED BIBLIOGRAPHY

Novels

Black Sunday (New York: Putnam, 1975; London: Hodder, 1975)

Red Dragon (New York: Putnam, 1981; London: The Bodley Head, 1981)

The Silence of the Lambs (New York: St Martin's, 1988; London: Heinemann, 1989)

Hannibal (New York: Delacorte Press, 1999; London: Heinemann, 1999)

Articles by Thomas Harris

'An Ideal English Class Syllabus for 9th Graders', *Mouth2Mouth*, (Issue 1, Spring 1994)

'Wild Dogs Howling in the Night ... and the Moment I Came Face to Face with Hannibal Lecter' (preface to forthcoming omnibus edition), *Mail on Sunday* (9 July 2000)

Audiobook

Hannibal, read by the author, Abridged by Lynn Lauber (Random House, 1999)

Films

Black Sunday, directed by John Frankenheimer (Paramount, 1977)

Manhunter, (*Red Dragon*), directed by Michael Mann (De Laurentiis Entertainment 1986)

The Silence of the Lambs, directed by Jonathan Demme. (Orion, 1991)

Hannibal, directed by Ridley Scott (Universal Pictures, 2001)

Articles about Thomas Harris

Phoebe Hoban: 'The Silence of the Writer' (*New York* 15 April 1991)

Paul Palmer: 'The Man Behind the Monster' (*Daily Mail* 13 June 1991)

Caroline Graham: 'The Silence of the Author' (*Mail on Sunday* 9 May 1999)

Joel Achenbach: 'Hannibal Author Thomas Harris, Toasting the Pleasures of the Flesh but Unwilling to Press It' (*Washington Post* 21 June 1999)

Meg Laughlin: 'The Silence of the Author' (*Tulsa World* 15 August 1999)

Selected Reviews

The Silence of the Lambs
Eric Griffiths: 'Fluttering on the Wings of Gothic Terror'
(*Sunday Correspondent* 1989)

Hannibal.
John Lanchester'Slapping the Clammy Flab' (*London Review of Books* 29 July 1999)
Martin Amis: 'Hannibal: The Camus of Carnage' (*Talk* September 1999)
Stephen King: 'Hannibal the Cannibal' (*New York Times* 13 June 1999)
Eric Griffiths: 'Food for Thought in the Godless World of a Serial Killer' (*Daily Telegraph* 8 June 1999)

Website

Dissecting *Hannibal*: www.geocities.com/hannotations/

AUTHOR BIOGRAPHY

David Sexton is the literary editor of the The London Evening Standard *and radio reviewer for* The Sunday Telegraph